The *Sound* of GOD'S APPLAUSE

The *Sound* of GOD'S APPLAUSE

Living a life that glorifies the Father

Les Hughes

BROADMAN
&HOLMAN
PUBLISHERS

Nashville, Tennessee

© 1999
by Les Hughes
All rights reserved
Printed in the United States of America

0–8054–1823–7

Published by Broadman & Holman Publishers, Nashville, Tennessee
Acquisitions and Development Editor: Leonard G. Goss
Page Design and Typesetting: TF Designs, Mount Juliet, Tennessee

Dewey Decimal Classification: 2248
Subject Heading: CHRISTIAN LIVING
Library of Congress Card Catalog Number: 98–47098

Unless otherwise noted, Scripture quotations are from the Holy Bible,
New International Version, © copyright 1973, 1978, 1984.
Other versions are marked NASB, the New American Standard Bible,
© Copyright The Lockman Foundation, 1960, 1962, 1963, 1968, 1971,
1972, 1973, 1975, 1977, 1995;
NKJV, New King James Version, copyright © 1979, 1980, 1982,
Thomas Nelson, Inc., Publishers.

Library of Congress Cataloging-in-Publication Data

Hughes, Les. 1960-
    The sound of God's applause : living a life that glorifies the
Father / Les Hughes.
        p. cm.
    ISBN 0–8054–1823–7 (pbk.)
    1. Christian life. 2. Social acceptance. I. Title.
BV4501.2.H787   1999
248.4—dc21
                                                             98–47098
                                                                  CIP

1 2 3 4 5 03 02 01 00 99

Dedicated to my wife,
Page,
my biggest fan, my greatest encourager,
and my best friend in this world.

Contents

❀❧❧❀

Acknowledgments

Please allow me to thank the following folks:

Del Fehsenfeld and his partners in ministry at Life Action Ministries: I never met Del, but his courage serves as a constant source of encouragement to me. His message on fear of man changed my life forever.

Leonard Goss: My editor and adviser throughout this process. From our very first discussion, he has enthusiastically given his support.

Broadman & Holman Publishers: Thanks for taking a chance on a young pup of an author.

Harold Bryson: Thanks for proofreading the manuscript and giving your wise counsel. Advice from an experienced author is as precious as nuggets of gold.

Bob Russell: Undershepherd at Southeast Christian Church in Louisville, Kentucky. You already know what your preaching ministry means to me. In times when I struggled to illustrate these precepts, you gave me just the right "nail" to hang a principle on. Thanks.

Kyle and Caleb: My two oldest sons. Thanks for holding Dad's feet to the fire to help my walk be consistent with my talk. My prayer is that you both always glorify your heavenly Father.

Luke and Gené: My youngest son and only daughter. Thanks for your innocence and childlike faith. Thanks for reminding us of Jesus' presence in every moment of every day. Your trust in Mom and Dad is an example of how we should trust our heavenly Father. My love for you is given as God's love is given to us—unconditionally.

Page: The most generous person I know. Thanks not only for your encouragement for me to write, but for fifteen wonderful years of marriage.

And thanks to you, the reader: You've taken a chance in purchasing this book. I hope you are blessed as you read it. My one desire is for you to experience the liberation of living a life that glorifies the Father. For most of you, we are meeting for the first time. I hope it isn't the last. To quote Rick Blaine, Humphrey Bogart's character in the film Casablanca, I hope this is "the beginning of a beautiful friendship."

To all of you: May your life always please the Lord. And may the sound of the Father's applause ring in your ears.

Les

Introduction

❧❧❧

At the funeral service of Richard M. Nixon, Billy Graham said, "There comes a time when we have to realize that life is short, and in the end the only thing that really counts is not how others see us here, but how God sees us and what the record books of Heaven have to say." I agree. That conviction is at the heart of this book.

Have you ever done something primarily for the approval of someone else? Join the club. Most of us have. Think of how many of our decisions are affected by what others think: the vehicle we drive, the clothes we wear, how we discipline our children, what schools our children attend, where we live, and even what church we attend.

Seeking the approval of others affects clergy and laity, politicians and constituents, teenagers and adults, women and men, outgoing people as well as shy. Sometimes seeking to please others brings no harm. But problems begin when we care more about what people think about us than what God thinks.

People are visible and God is invisible, so we tend to react to the visible and the immediate: what do others think? Sometimes being concerned over what others think of us is good. Positive peer pressure can motivate us to do good deeds, such as give to the needy and be kind to others. Those benevolent deeds are admired in our society. Regardless of our motivation, the results are positive.

But people-pleasing does not always have positive results. Seeking the approval of others can become burdensome or even

1

oppressive. As I began research for this book, I was amazed to discover the wide range of people who were affected by this same phenomenon. I talked with many people who appeared to have their act together. Many admitted that they act out of concern for what others think of them.

Even a respected leader like former New Jersey Senator Bill Bradley was not immune to the fear of what others thought about him and his leadership. In his book, *Time Present, Time Past,* he confessed how a near loss in his reelection campaign of 1990 changed him forever.

Prior to the election, he tried to be cautious regarding controversial issues to avoid offending individuals and groups. Later he wrote about the freedom he felt when he started speaking and acting out of the convictions of his heart:

> A senator's job is to pass laws, and much of my legislative efforts had gone to righting wrongs through big reform, but the job has another dimension—using the platform of the office to speak, to challenge, to lead. In the latter category, I had failed, because until after the 1990 election I had not used the potential of my office to confront Americans with the tough choices of our day. I had not waded into turbulent waters by defining my views clearly, preferring instead the comfort of ambiguity or silence. . . . For much of my career I had no authentic political voice. I had been campaigning all over the country not to change the world or shake up my audiences but to please the roomful of people to whom I was speaking [italics mine]. The issues I championed did not move people. [To] the public at large I was a blank slate. . . .
>
> I had reasoned that if I didn't polarize people, I could more easily build a legislative coalition. But passing laws and mobilizing a country require different styles. Until 1991, when I began to speak from my gut as well as my head, I had been content to follow a nonconfrontational strategy that had always allowed me to achieve my goals. I was smooth, not sharp-edged; bland, not "exciting." . . . As a result, my words rarely had the ring of truth to the nonpolitical observer.[1]

I appreciate Senator Bradley's honesty. Maybe you can relate. Bradley probably speaks for many others. A business person feels the pressure of doing what is right over gaining the favor of a superior. An educator wants to keep her position, but the textbook from which she teaches holds a theory contrary to her beliefs. She cannot ignore the sweeping impact her decisions will make in the lives of others.

A mother and father refuse to allow inappropriate or immoral behavior, but they do not wish to make their child angry with discipline. A pastor feels guilty because he's gradually compromised his convictions so he'll be liked by his colleagues and parishioners. After all, he doesn't want to be labeled an intolerant radical. But has he compromised God's Word?

A physician values the life of every human being, both born and unborn, and refuses to perform abortions. Her convictions are not held by some in her profession. How can she follow her convictions against abortion and still have the respect of her peers or remain on the hospital staff?

These issues are complex. The difficulties involved can create anxiety and stress in the life of a Christian. When a believer chooses to seek God's approval, he or she may experience criticism from others. In more extreme cases, obedience to God may lead to persecution.

Seeking the approval of others instead of our heavenly Father leads to guilt, frustration, conflict, spiritual oppression, and perhaps divine discipline. But Christians don't have to experience this conflict. We can take heart. Many courageous people are winning this internal conflict every day.

I already mentioned Senator Bradley's admission of his personal struggle. Let's go to the other side of Capitol Hill for some insight from someone who discovered the rewards of pleasing God rather than people. Oklahoma Congressman J. C. Watts, at the 1997 Southern Baptist Convention Pastor's Conference in Dallas, Texas, said:

> I do not apologize for my personal, intimate relationship with Jesus Christ. . . . We've got some press here and that's OK. You can write what you want to write. You can say what you want to say tomorrow morning in the papers about what Congressman Watts said. And you can say what Congressman Watts said and

what he talked about, and you can go back to the fourth district of Oklahoma, and you can send the press release down there. . . . Let me tell you something, folks. I don't need to be a congressman to tell me who I am or what I should stand for. I don't need "Congressman" in front of my name. I take a whole lot more pride in being called "Daddy" than I do in being called "Congressman."

I will say what I want to say. I will do what I want to do, because I don't need this job! God had me working before I went to Washington, and I'll be working when I leave Washington. Don't worry about me.

I had a call back in 1994 [when] I chose to run for Congress. I had a reporter out of Washington that called me and talked to me for about thirty minutes, and then he finally got around to asking me the sixty-four-thousand-dollar question.

He said, "Commissioner," (I was a commissioner in state government at the time), "Commissioner, let me ask you—are you going to accept the help of the Christian right?" And I kind of chuckled, and I said, "Since you put it like that, I'm a minister. I am the Christian right."[2]

Mr. Watts took a big step toward being liberated from the bondage of pleasing others.

Perhaps you grapple with whether to seek the approval of God or the applause of people. Do you ever feel insecure about what someone thinks about you? Do you ever feel intimidated or overwhelmed at work, in your home, or in your service to the Lord? Have you felt insecure in your walk with Christ and relationships with other people? Do you ever refrain from doing the right thing because you're afraid of how people will react? Do you worry about your reputation? Your finances? Your success? If so, don't you want to be freed from those concerns? I believe we can be, but not on our own. We need help.

Unfortunately, I haven't always acted with the same courage as Congressman Watts. My guess is that he has moments of weakness just like the rest of us. The solution to the struggle of seeking human approval is the heart of this book. In our study together, we will discover how to overcome our preoccupation with pleasing people so we can instead seek God's approval.

Specifically, we will examine the ministry of Jesus of Nazareth. Instead of allowing his actions to be determined by others, he focused on doing the will of the One who sent him. In the life of Jesus, God called the shots.

My own pilgrimage in this area began in October 1995. The church where I served experienced a two-week crusade under the leadership of Life Action Ministries. I anticipated God doing a unique work in the church. He didn't disappoint me. One morning during the crusade, our staff met with the Life Action team leaders to view a videotape. The message on the video was given by Del Fehsenfeld. The topic was "Fear of Man," a phrase based on Proverbs 29:25: "Fear of man will prove to be a snare, but whoever trusts in the LORD is kept safe."

Del founded Life Action Ministries and died at the age of forty-three. He exchanged a brain tumor for his crown of glory only months prior to our viewing the video. At the time that Del presented the message he knew he was dying. He lived for only a few weeks after he gave the address.

I consider myself a bold preacher—not abrasive or obnoxious—just confident, not fearful. My wife has an uncle who periodically says, "That scares me, and I ain't scared of nothin'." I pastored three different churches over a period of ten years and was willing to address practically anything from the pulpit.

Under the leadership of the Holy Spirit I had tackled some difficult issues, such as divorce and remarriage, abortion, creation and evolution, homosexuality, and the role of men and women in the family. So why did this idea of the fear of man disturb me?

I began to ask myself some hard questions. In my preaching was I seeking the approval of God, or did I want to hear people say, "That was a good sermon, Pastor"? I realized I had mistaken my boldness from the pulpit for seeking God's approval only. Then I viewed Fehsenfeld's address. He gave one of the characteristics of a person who seeks to please others: "He is able to confront corporately but not privately." Bull's-eye!

So I began to ask God to change me. I wanted to revere him more than any human being. I wanted a holy fear and reverence for him to be manifested in my behavior and in my pastoral leadership. More than the approval of others, I wanted to hear God say, "Well done, good and faithful servant." I wanted to hear the sound of God's applause.

As a child of God, I longed to hear the same words Jesus heard: "This is my beloved Son, in whom I am well pleased." I desired the courage shown by the three Hebrew young men facing the fiery furnace that enabled them to say, "If we are thrown into the blazing furnace, the God we serve is able to save us from it, and he will rescue us from your hand, O king. But even if he does not, we want you to know, O king, that we will not serve your gods or worship the image of gold you have set up" (Dan. 3:17–18).

In his book, The Handwriting on the Wall, David Jeremiah tells about Studdard Kennedy, who was a chaplain during World War II. On several occasions Kennedy was shoved into the front lines of battle. The places where he ministered often placed his life in jeopardy. One day, while traveling through France, he wrote a letter to his ten-year-old son back home:

> The first prayer I want my son to say for me is not "God, keep Daddy safe," but "God, make Daddy brave. And if he has hard things to do, make him strong to do them."
>
> Son, life and death don't matter. But right and wrong do. Daddy dead is Daddy still, but Daddy dishonored before God is something too awful for words. I suppose you would like to put in a bit about safety, too, and Mother would like that, I'm sure. Well, put it in afterwards, for it really doesn't matter nearly as much as doing the right thing.[3]

Wouldn't you like to experience the freedom that comes from knowing you are marching to the beat of the divine drummer? I hope the contents of this book will help you do that. I'm now in a university setting, and my pilgrimage has just begun. Hopefully, you will benefit from some of the things I've noticed about people who discovered the secret of pleasing God rather than people.

I know this concept of pleasing God instead of people goes against popular thinking, but most of the Bible goes counterculture. In addition to looking at some biblical accounts throughout our journey together, I will include examples of people throughout history and in our day who sought the approval of God over the approval of others. Some may be familiar; others will not be. Some were rewarded on earth and some were ridiculed, but all received the greatest blessing of all—the approval of their heavenly Father.

A few years ago I saw an interview (on one of the network prime time television shows) with a special lady who seemed to want God's approval over the applause of people. At the time of the interview, Mrs. Ozzie Wattleton was living in Atlanta.

A couple of details about Mrs. Wattleton made the interview especially interesting to me. For starters, Ozzie is the mother of Faye Wattleton, who was the president of Planned Parenthood at the time. The younger Ms. Wattleton was, and is an outspoken advocate for the pro-choice movement.

Another matter that made Ozzie Wattleton unique was her profession. She was a minister of the gospel of Jesus Christ. In the report, television cameras followed this stately African-American woman as she walked up and down the streets of Atlanta. She was both elegant and down-to-earth. People recognized her, called out to her, and waved in her direction.

Their admiration for her was not based on the visibility or celebrity status of her daughter, Faye. The citizens of the inner city of Atlanta love Miss Ozzie because she has dedicated her life to serving them and to spreading the gospel with grace and truth.

In this television interview, instead of focusing on Ozzie's service to her community, the interviewer concentrated on the many differences between Ozzie and her daughter Faye concerning matters of morality, especially on the sensitive issue of abortion. Ozzie made no bones about it—she was pro-life.

I'll never forget the gracious way Ozzie Wattleton handled the tough questions. She was honest about her convictions and admitted many of her beliefs differed from her daughter's.

The reporter continued her probe, asking how the two strong-willed ladies handled family gatherings and occasions that could lead to disagreements or even conflicts between them. Ozzie said something like this: "We've talked and debated so much about those issues. She knows where I stand, and I know where she stands. We've gotten to the point now, we just accept that there are some topics we just need to avoid discussing. We're never going to see eye to eye." She had an obvious peace about her life and her convictions.

Then as the interview was coming to a close, the reporter made one final statement to Ozzie. She said, in a rather patronizing way, "Now, Miss Ozzie, you know some of your opinions are pretty old-fashioned. After all, these are the 1980s. Holding to these beliefs is not going to win you any popularity contests."

Ozzie calmly looked at the interviewer and smiled. She gave the young reporter a look and smile that communicated, "Child, if you only knew what I know. You have a long life to live and many lessons to learn." But Ozzie didn't attempt to embarrass the reporter.

Instead, she leaned forward, her white hair serving as a mantle of wisdom, and calmly, yet confidently, said something like this: "Young lady, you're right. Some of these views are pretty old-fashioned. Holding these convictions won't win any popularity contests for me." Then she added, "But Miss Ozzie ain't runnin'."

I loved it. What a great attitude—to be able to say, "I'm not trying to impress the world. I'm not even trying to win the approval of my family members. I just want to serve the Lord and seek his approval. I won't win any popularity contests, but I'm not running."

If you want to experience the liberation that was demonstrated in the life of Jesus Christ and in the experiences of people like Ozzie Waddleton, and scores of others, join me as we dig in to God's Word together.

Chapter 1
In Need of Approval

Do not work for food that spoils, but for food that endures
to eternal life, which the Son of Man will give you.
On him God the Father has placed his seal of approval.
(John 6:27)

The term used in the Bible for seeking to please people rather than God is "fear of man." In the Fourth Gospel, John told about some people who rejected Jesus because they were afraid of the consequences: "Yet at the same time many even among the leaders believed in him. But because of the Pharisees they would not confess their faith for fear they would be put out of the synagogue; for they loved praise from men more than praise from God" (John 12:42–43).

In the first century, banishment from the synagogue was a serious matter. People who were excommunicated from the synagogue were ostracized from society. To these orthodox Jewish rulers, banishment from their religion was too high a price to be disciples of Jesus. William Barclay wrote,

> It has been said and said truly that secret discipleship is a contradiction in terms for, "either the secrecy kills the discipleship, or the discipleship kills the secrecy. . . .
> [Banishment from the synagogue] was too high a price to pay. So they lived a lie because they were not big enough to stand up for the truth. . . .
>
> They preferred to stand well with men rather than with God. They thought far more of what men thought of them than of what God thought of them.[1]

In other words, a person is affected by fear of man when she is concerned more with how she is perceived by human beings than with how she is viewed by God. The Bible has a word for substituting something in God's place—idolatry.

According to Del Fehsenfeld, founder of Life Action Ministries, the presence or absence of fear of man is a matter of personal security or insecurity. For example, insecurity comes as a result of placing confidence and trust in people and things that can be taken away. Think for a moment just how futile and unproductive this thinking is.

What would our lives be like if our actions were controlled by what others think of us or how others behave toward us? Imagine your life if your sense of worth was determined by the encouragement of another, or lack of encouragement. Your self-esteem would go up and down like a yo-yo. You would have no sense of security.

Now think of the opposite of insecurity. Real security comes from placing our faith and trust in that which cannot be taken away from us—namely the presence and love of God demonstrated in its various forms. We can boil down every reason for seeking God's approval instead of the approval of others to this: "Some trust in chariots and some in horses, but we trust in the name of the LORD our God" (Ps. 20:7).

Here are some examples of how seeking approval primarily from people can lead to insecurity. If a church leader places all his faith and trust in the church, he is devastated when criticism comes from church members. When an employee places all her faith and trust in her boss and the employer shows no encouragement, the worker becomes discouraged and her morale drops. If a parent's only gauge of worth is in a relationship with a child and the child rebels, the parent may feel worthless.

Please allow me to pause here in order to admit that without the power of God there are plenty of things to fear in this world:

 ❧ Being fired by an ungodly employer for refusing to compromise your integrity in the marketplace.

11

❧ Losing your job as a schoolteacher for allowing Christian principles to affect how you approach some subject matter.

❧ Being accused of child abuse because you try to follow the biblical guidelines of loving discipline.

❧ Having your reputation hurt by a gossip who has an ax to grind.

❧ Losing an election because your beliefs go contrary to the voters' opinions.

Let's face it, without the promise that "we are more than conquerors through him who loved us" (Rom. 8:37), fear and insecurity are legitimate responses to all of these and other threats. You could come up with your own list.

But take heart. God has provided a cure for our uncertainty. The cure for this insecurity is to place our faith, trust, and confidence in that which cannot be taken away. Fehsenfeld told of two things no one can take away from you: your relationship with God through Jesus Christ and your relationship with his Word.

In our pilgrimage together, we're going to discover how our relationship with God and his Word can give us real security. We'll observe ways to seek God's applause instead of the favor of people. "Fear of man will prove to be a snare, but whoever trusts in the LORD is kept safe, (Prov. 29:25, emphasis mine). Did you see it? Seeking human approval leads to insecurity. It is a snare. Trusting in God leads to real security.[2]

People's Opinions Do Matter

Before we press on, please let me say I'm not advocating a cavalier attitude with regard to others' perception of you. A person who seeks to please God does not have this kind of attitude, "I don't care what people think of me. I'm going to do my own thing no matter what." Some people are just belligerent—not because of their allegiance to the will of God, but out of pride and self-centeredness.

People like Madonna and Dennis Rodman seem to thrive on controversy. They say, "I don't care what people think. I've got to be me." MTV advertisers encourage teenagers and young adults to question authority. "Don't conform to be what society says you should be," they say.

Our Christian testimony is determined in part by our sensitivity to the thoughts and attitudes of others. The apostle Paul wrote, "If it is possible, as far as it depends on you, live at peace with everyone" (Rom. 12:18).

Jesus grew in wisdom and stature, "finding favor with God and men" (Luke 2:52). The first-century Christians enjoyed the favor of people, and the Lord added to their number daily (Acts 2:47). In other words, modern believers should be aware of perceptions of others. How others see you may affect their attitude about Christ. Concern about the opinions of others only becomes a problem when our concern over what people think causes us to act contrary to God's will for us.

One rainy afternoon, my wife Page took all but one of our children to lunch with her parents. They lived only twenty minutes away. One of our older children wanted to stay home. Since I was just a few minutes away at the office, we let him stay. I had to speak at a business luncheon, but I told him after I finished speaking I would bring him a video game to play while he was home. The only instructions we gave him were to lock the doors and stay inside until his mother or I got home.

By the time I got to the house, the rain had stopped. I was walking toward the door when I heard, "Hey, Dad," from the other side of the yard. He was coming from the direction of the road. I said, "Son, did your mom tell you not to go out of the house?" He meekly replied, "Yes, sir, but my friend begged me to go with him to walk their dog. He begged me, Dad." He feared rejection from the friend more than discipline from his mother and me.

I calmly said, "Son, you have directly disobeyed the instructions of your mother and me. Go into the house, I have to

13

discipline you." His heart was truly broken, and so was mine. I told him the reasons we had given him the prohibition—not to take away his fun, but for his own protection and safety. The instructions were for his own good, even if they didn't make sense to him.

I explained there could come a time when a fear of discipline might save his life. I wanted him to understand, but it was hard for him to be objective. Someday he will understand better and appreciate us more, but he has to live until that day comes to understand our actions better. Right now, what's important is that he obeys and respects our judgment.

God's Commands Matter More

Sometimes God's commands don't make sense either. "Joshua, march monotonously around that wall." "Noah, build an ark." "A what, Lord?" "An ark, Noah." "What's an ark, Lord?" "Something to protect your family from the rain." "What's rain, Lord?" "Just build the ark, Noah."

Need more examples? God instructed Adam and Eve not to eat of a luscious-looking fruit. He gave orders through Elisha to Naaman to wash seven times in the Jordan. He told Gideon to reduce his army to a fraction of what Gideon thought he needed. These commands made little sense at the time, but God had unique reasons for giving the instructions.

He also has sufficient reasons for his instructions to us. For example, we are to worship no other gods except him because he is the only one who can save us and provide for us. All other objects of worship are dead.

We are not to commit murder because life is God's sacred creation. Without this prohibition, no one would be safe and society would crumble.

We are to remain faithful to our own spouse so that the home is stable and families are strong. God has plenty of reasons for wanting us to seek his approval.

Following God's commands may even add years to your life: "The fear of the LORD adds length to life, but the years of the wicked are cut short" (Prov. 10:27). Want to stick around for a while? Revere God and be obedient to him.

We have the capacity to understand some of God's commands, but others we may never understand. Our responsibility is to remain obedient anyway. If we act obediently out of a holy reverence for the Lord now, we will be protected until the day we are mature enough to understand fully. Sometimes God reveals the rationale. When he does, be grateful. However, if he doesn't tell us why, our obedience will bring his blessing.

I will probably never understand fully Abraham's willingness to sacrifice his precious son Isaac. That divine command couldn't have made complete sense to Abraham. Do you remember the result of Abraham's obedience?

Just as Abraham was ready to thrust the knife into the flesh of his son, the angel of the Lord called out and said, "'Abraham! Abraham! . . . Do not lay a hand on the boy,' he said. 'Do not do anything to him. Now I know that you fear God, because you have not withheld from me your son, your only son.'" (Gen. 22:11–12).

Then the angel added this declaration from the Lord: "I swear by myself, declares the LORD, that because you have done this and have not withheld your son, your only son, I will surely bless you and make your descendants as numerous as the stars in the sky and as the sand on the seashore. Your descendants will take possession of the cities of their enemies, and through your offspring all nations on earth will be blessed, because you have obeyed me" (Gen. 22:16–18, emphasis mine).

The individuals whose lives have glorified the Father share one common trait: they overcame their need for human approval so they could be obedient to God. With divine help you can, too. They were imperfect human beings. They were flawed just like we are. They had moments of insecurity just like you do, but the same God who helped them will give you and me the same victory.

So let's begin our journey. Our first stop will be to look into the mirror. Let's examine why we even care about what others think.

Chapter 2
Where Does the Need for Approval Come From?

God knows your hearts. What is highly valued among men is detestable in God's sight. (Luke 16:15)

They were not confessing Him, lest they should be put out of the synagogue; for they loved the approval of men rather than the approval of God. (John 12:42b–43, NASB)

The Approval of Parents

Most human beings seek approval and acceptance from early childhood. For many, the quest for approval continues as long as they live. Our longing for the blessing of others begins with a desire for the approval of our parents.

One evening, Page and I were saying our bedtime prayers with the children, and Caleb, then nine years old, volunteered to lead us. (He had a big baseball game the next morning and he knew a little divine assistance could only help his cause).

As Caleb neared the conclusion of his prayer, he said, "And dear Lord, please help me do well in my game tomorrow so my dad will be impressed, 'cause I want my dad to be impressed with me." I felt so small. I think I could have walked tiptoe under a dachshund.

Had I given my son the impression that he had to earn my approval? I'm proud of him no matter what. When he finished his prayer by saying, "Amen," I said, "Caleb, I'm always impressed with you." My approval was important to him.

In over ten years of pastoral ministry, I witnessed the behavior of people whose need for approval had not been satisfied during those childhood or teenage years. They tried to make up for the approval deficiency as adults. The names and specifics differed, but the plots were similar: "My achievements were never enough for my mom/dad. If I got an A on a test my mom would ask, 'How many people scored higher than you?' If I scored one touchdown, my dad would say, 'You should have scored two.' My best was never good enough."

John Trent wrote about Brian, who never felt the joy of his father's approval. Driven by his father, a retired Marine officer, to be a successful Marine, Brian fell short of his father's dreams. After Brian received a dishonorable discharge from the Corps because of incorrigibility, his father cut off contact with Brian. His dad gave him the silent treatment for years.

After years of rejection, Brian received a telephone call from his mother telling him his father had suffered a heart attack. Brian immediately flew half-way across the country to be at his father's side. During the flight he hoped to be reconciled finally with his father and hear those special words: "I love you. I'm proud of you."

By the time Brian arrived at the hospital, his dad had slipped into a coma. Brian begged the motionless figure in the bed, "Dad, please wake up! Please say that you love me, please!" Brian's weeping could be heard down the hallway of the hospital, but his father never woke up.[1]

Why do we seek that kind of approval? We say the opinion of others really doesn't matter, but deep down we know better. Our actions and emotions betray our words.

How are we to respond to this need for applause that we possess? How can we manage it? Should we ignore its existence?

18

Should people feel guilty for desiring approval? Are we showing no backbone when we wonder how our actions are going to affect someone's opinion of us?

From where does this drive for approval come? Why do we care what someone thinks about us? Is the need for approval just another result of the spiritual fall of humanity from the grace of God? Is this need just one more example of how we fall short of God's standard?

Our Need for Approval Comes from God

The need for approval in itself is not a sin. This desire was placed inside of us by God so we might seek *his* blessing. Paul encouraged Timothy to "be diligent to present yourself *approved to God* as a workman who does not need to be ashamed, handling accurately the word of truth" (2 Tim. 2:15, emphasis mine).

Jesus was driven by his primary mission to please the Father and to do his will. His passion was to glorify God. In other words, our Lord was one who sought approval, but his constant need for approval was a healthy condition—a need for the approval of God.

The Gospel writers clearly tell that Jesus heard the sound of God's applause. In fact, God affirmed his approval of Jesus in at least three different ways. One way the Father demonstrated his approval of his Son was audibly. Jesus heard God's approval spoken by the Father at his baptism when God acknowledged, "You are my Son, whom I love; with you I am well pleased" (Mark 1:11; see also Matt. 3:17 and Luke 3:22).

The word used by Matthew, Mark, and Luke to describe the Father's pleasure with the Son is *eudokeo*, a word describing one's favour resting on another. In other words, the pleasure of the Father rests on those who fulfill his purpose and do his will.

The second way God demonstrated his pleasure toward his Son was by allowing Jesus to witness miracles and be used as God's instrument in performing wonderful signs. In John 9,

Jesus healed a man who had been born blind, but Jesus' opponents questioned the source of Jesus' power. The man who had been healed replied, "But if anyone is God-fearing, and does His will, He hears him" (John 9:31b, NASB).

Jesus himself considered these miracles to be evidence to the crowds that he had been sent by the Father. For example, when Jesus appealed to God for Lazarus to be raised, he prayed, "Father, I thank you that you have heard me. I knew that you always hear me, but I said this for the benefit of the people standing here, that they may believe that you sent me" (John 11:41–42).

A third way the Father showed his approval of his Son was demonstrated in the resurrection of Christ. After Jesus was raised, Peter and the apostles were ordered to stop preaching in the name of Christ. The disciples ignored the orders of the religious leaders and were brought before a puzzled Sanhedrin.

The authorities rebuked the disciples again for teaching in the name of Jesus. Peter's and the apostles' reply was simple: "We must obey God rather than men! The God of our fathers raised Jesus from the dead—whom you had killed by hanging him on a tree. God exalted him to his own right hand as Prince and Savior that he might give repentance and forgiveness of sins to Israel" (Acts 5:29–31).

So these followers of Jesus considered the resurrection of the Lord both an affirmation of God's approval of his Son and incentive for them to obey God rather than people. The reply of the apostles to the council may be stated another way: "The worse thing you can do to us is to kill us like you did Jesus, but God undid your malicious actions. God raised him from the dead. Now if we have to choose whether we will obey God or you, we will obey God. We desire *his* approval, not yours."

Sound familiar? Jesus phrased the same conviction this way: "Do not be afraid of those who kill the body but cannot kill the soul. Rather, be afraid of the One who can destroy both soul and body in hell" (Matt. 10:28).

How Do We Handle Our Desire for Approval?

To summarize, the answer is not to ignore our desire for approval and acceptance. The solution is not to seek rejection from people, assuming that rejection from people equates approval from God. Our need for approval is not evil, it's healthy. It's God-given. This need for approval can only be fulfilled completely by him. When we get to the point that God's opinion of us is more important than the opinions of human beings, we have satisfied our need for approval in a healthy manner.

G. Cambell Morgan, along with 149 other young men, was seeking entrance into the Wesleyan ministry in 1888. He passed the doctrinal examinations and began to prepare for his trial sermon. When the crucial day came, Morgan stepped behind the pulpit of the one-thousand-seat auditorium and preached to three ministers and seventy-five others who came to listen.

Two weeks after preaching the sermon, Campbell's name appeared on a list along with 104 others who had been rejected for the ministry that year. Morgan sent a telegram to his father that contained one word: "Rejected." His diary entry that day read: "Very dark everything seems. Still, He knoweth best."

His father's brief response came quickly and serves as an encouragement for those of us who long for the approval of our heavenly Father. His message read: "Rejected on Earth. Accepted in heaven. Dad."[2]

Whether you are the President of the United States or a nobody in the world's eyes, in the final analysis, God's opinion of us is what really matters. He alone can see into the deepest places of our souls. He isn't fooled by appearances. He isn't duped by an attractive veneer.

Remember, "The LORD does not look at the things man looks at. Man looks at the outward appearance, but the LORD looks at the heart" (1 Sam. 16:7b–8). When our heavenly Father looks into your heart, what does he see? Someone who longs for his pleasure, or someone who hungers for the approval of others?

21

Chapter 3
Am I Seeking the Approval of People?

I, even I, am he who comforts you.
Who are you that you fear mortal men? (Isa. 51:12)

The angel of the LORD encamps around those
who fear him, and he delivers them. (Ps. 34:7)

How do we determine whom we are living to please? Are there ways to measure whether we function to please God or to please human beings? In Del Fehsenfeld's address mentioned earlier, he gave several evidences of human insecurity. Gaining an understanding of these evidences will aid in identifying whose applause you seek.

The following is an expansion of Fehsenfeld's list. To determine whether you are seeking to please your heavenly Father or others, ask yourself the following questions.

Am I Preoccupied with the Opinions of Others?

When I accomplish something, large or small, is one of my first thoughts what other people think of the achievement, or do I say in my heart, "Lord, was that OK? It's *your* approval I long for"?

Let's look at a couple of examples from the Bible. Noah and Simon Peter both warned their listeners to repent and turn to God. The only people who responded to Noah's message were his own family members. Peter had more encouraging results. Over three thousand people took heed to Peter's instructions.

Today Noah would be considered a failure, and Peter would be leading church growth conferences. But weren't they both obedient to God's instructions? Hadn't they done what he commanded? Our success is not determined by the response of people, but by our obedience to the Lord.

With regard to Paul the apostle's success, he wrote, "I planted the seed, Apollos watered it, but God made it grow" (1 Cor. 3:6). The results of our obedience are up to God. Our sense of gratification in any accomplishment should come because we are obedient, not because we are liked or accepted by others.

The psalmist wrote, "Blessed are all who fear the LORD, who walk in his ways. You will eat the fruit of your labor; blessings and prosperity will be yours" (Ps. 128:1–2). God blesses those who march to the beat of his drum.

Krystle Newquist, a fourteen-year-old Little League softball player from Lemont, Illinois, was determined to stand by her convictions no matter what others thought of her.

According to CNN reporter, Lisa Price, Krystle was made to sit on the bench and not play in games, because she covered up the team sponsor's name on her jersey with duct tape. She refused to advertise on her body the name of a local bar, in part because her grandfather died of cirrhosis. The disease causes the liver to degenerate and is often associated with alcohol.

Krystle wasn't just determined to be a "rebellious teen." She asked league officials to allow her to play on another team. The officials told her she was too late. The softball season had already started.

Krystle even offered to buy her team new uniforms out of her graduation money, but the league said no. The bottom line for the league seemed to be that they wanted the money from the sponsors.

Krystle was not bitter. She still sat on the bench and cheered her team on for the rest of the season. But the matter was not up for debate as far as she was concerned.[1] I'll guarantee you this. Krystle's courage will take her farther in life than conforming to the league would have.

Krystle couldn't have taken her courageous stand if she was preoccupied with what others thought about her. How much do you think about what others think? Do their opinions of you cause you not to act when you know you should? Do their opinions motivate you to do something you know is wrong? If we are going to be freed from the opinions of others, we must first be honest about our own condition.

Do I Confront Corporately, but Not Personally?

For many years of ministry I wasn't aware of how often I was affected by what others thought of me. My condition was concealed by my willingness to tackle tough issues when I talked to a group of people. I reasoned, "If I were intimidated, I certainly wouldn't deal with a difficult subject in front of scores of people."

For example, consider the differences of the following comparison. Suppose I say from the pulpit, "According to Scripture, the husband is to be the spiritual leader of a marriage relationship." Many evangelical Christians would agree with the principle.

Now let's be more specific. Suppose as pastor I notice a wife of a church leader who possesses a bitter or critical spirit. Her bitterness begins to affect her husband's leadership in a negative way. If I love that brother, I will approach him and honestly say, "You need to show some spiritual leadership in your home. Your wife is beginning to hurt your leadership in the church."

Believe me, the latter personal approach would be more difficult than the former impersonal method. More courage is needed for the second approach. It's personal, but the personal appeal is more effective than the corporate.

I know what you're thinking: "That's too risky. I'd become vulnerable." You're absolutely right. Our fear of how a person may respond has to be outweighed by two factors.

First, our love for the individual has to be greater than our fear of their response. If we truly love that man, we will share with him our concern and help him to overcome the problem. I must confess, I have rarely loved at that level.

The second factor is our commitment to being obedient as God's undershepherds and servants. If we are obedient to God's instructions we will, with gentleness, correct "those who are in opposition, if perhaps God may grant them repentance leading to the knowledge of the truth" (2 Tim. 2:25, NASB).

James wrote, "My brothers, if one of you should wander from the truth and someone should bring him back, remember this: Whoever turns a sinner from the error of his way will save him from death and cover over a multitude of sins" (James 5:19–20).

Perhaps you try to avoid confrontation by telling yourself, "I'm not going to try to remove a speck from another's eye since I have a log in my own. I have my own faults. I can't point the finger at someone else." This attitude does not reflect the spirit of Jesus' instructions in Matthew 7. Jesus told his audience to *remove* the plank in their own eye so they could *see clearly* to remove the speck in another person's eye.

Some of you may be thinking: *"I'm not the Holy Spirit. It's not my job to convict."* True, but if we truly love someone and see the person behaving in a dangerous manner, will we not throw her a life preserver? To not react when a person is in peril is cruel indeed.

Do I Become Self-Conscious, Paranoid, or Intimidated Easily?

One pessimistic message on a bumper sticker read, "It's as bad as you think and they ARE out to get you." Rarely is that true. Most of us would be disappointed if we realized just how little people really do think about us. Self-consciousness and paranoia are often manifestations of pride in a person's life.

For example, if you are in a room full of people and see a group of folks huddled together, do you believe they are talking about you? Or do you assume that people are laughing at your expense? If so, you are demonstrating a symptom of the "fear of man." Furthermore, does your concern lead to a change in your behavior that would be inconsistent with God's instructions to his children?

Let's go back to the group setting mentioned above. This scenario is not hypothetical for scores of teenagers in our nation. Suppose a young teen is at a party and he observes most people drinking alcohol, some heavily. Our young person has made a vow to the Lord to be a total abstainer, not because the Bible says, "Thou shalt not drink," but because he believes his Christian witness would be affected negatively by drinking alcohol. Furthermore, drinking at his age is against the law.

The others at the party begin to poke fun and ridicule. The pressure grows. He becomes self-conscious regarding the opinions of others. He desires their approval. He wants to be accepted. Finally he compromises his convictions and gives in to the pressure. His need for approval is satisfied, but at what cost?

Out of intimidation and peer pressure he succumbs. He makes a decision not based on his vow to God, but on the "fear of man." After giving in, the teen must deal next with the guilt of going back on a vow he made to the Lord.

In a nutshell, the teen placed more value on the opinions of human beings than on keeping his vow to the Lord. "It is better not to vow than to make a vow and not fulfill it" (Eccles. 5:5).

Am I Defensive or Antagonistic When I Am Criticized, Rejected, or Corrected?

Defensive and antagonistic responses to criticism are symptoms of people pleasers. When you and I become defensive or antagonistic, we announce to the critic, "I put so much stock in your opinion of me and my actions, that your criticism of me is how I judge my value. Your opinion of me causes my worth as a person to diminish, therefore I am defensive."

In contrast to this inappropriate response to criticism, consider God's counsel: "A wise son heeds his father's instruction, but a mocker does not listen to rebuke" (Prov. 13:1). "A fool shows his annoyance at once, but a prudent man overlooks an insult" (Prov. 12:16). In other words, if the criticism is accurate, make the appropriate changes, but if the criticism is groundless, overlook the offense. "A man's discretion makes him slow to anger, And it is his glory to overlook a transgression" (Prov. 19:11, NASB).

Sometimes a wise and appropriate reaction to constructive criticism is to listen and respond accordingly. Coaching Little League baseball offers lots of challenges and opportunities to learn. Some boys and girls are easier to coach than others. Their response to instruction often depends on their perception of a criticism, which is really all instruction is—constructive criticism.

For example, I may tell one of the little future big-leaguers that he threw the ball to the wrong base or that she should have gotten in front of the ball instead of trying to field it to the side, or that he needs to catch the ball with both hands, or that she needs to swing at the ball when it comes over the plate instead of watching it go by. If the player believes I am picking on him, or I'm angry with her, the shoulders slump and the head drops, and it's not a good scene.

On the other hand, when the players know the coach is trying to help them, and when they realize that the criticism is instruction, not just faultfinding, their attitudes usually are completely different. They want to improve. They want to learn. They understand that the criticism is not a reflection of their value as a person; it is a result of a deficiency or shortcoming that can be corrected.

When someone criticizes you, try to be honest and discerning. The critic may be trying to help you. If you were to go to your physician for a checkup and the doctor found a lump, what would you want your physician to do? Ignore it, or treat you so you could get well? Most of us would want to get well.

If people close to us see glaring character flaws or mistakes we make or behavior inconsistent with the principles of Scripture, they should correct us. If they love us enough they will. When they do, be open to their instruction. Like the physician's scalpel, it may hurt at first, but healing will come as a result.

When criticism needs to be addressed (for example when the welfare of a church or family is at stake, or when a serious matter of integrity is in question), one may confront the accuser in a nondefensive way. An inaccurate accusation or criticism may be corrected with clarification.

But if you are being rejected or criticized for being obedient to the call of Christ, the Lord has this advice: "He who listens to you listens to me; he who rejects you rejects me; but he who rejects me rejects him who sent me" (Luke 10:16).

If our primary goal is to please the Lord, and we are doing *his* will, why should we be defensive? If someone gets angry because you're living in a manner to please your heavenly Father, that person needs to take the issue up with the Lord.

Believe me, when we are doing what God has called us to do, we will evoke criticism. Go ahead and expect it. Get ready for it, because it will come. When it does, be grateful. Jesus said, "Woe to you when all men speak well of you, for that is how their fathers treated the false prophets" (Luke 6:26). I once heard someone say when you and I are criticized for doing right, it gets the "woe" off our back.

Do I Have to Retain Control Over Others Most of the Time?

The need some people have to control others and their circumstances is another manifestation of a need for human approval and a mistrust of God. In other words, we try to control others because we believe they cannot handle conditions on their own. We fear that others will mess up their lives, so we volunteer to help, even when our help is not wanted.

Our desire to control comes not only from assuming that others can't handle their own circumstances but from believing that God needs our help, too. We say we trust his sovereignty, but our actions indicate otherwise. According to his Word, his plans are best. "Many are the plans in a man's heart, but the counsel of the LORD, it will stand" (Prov. 19:21, NASB).

If God ever had a bad day, which he doesn't, his worst counsel is better than the wisest advice from a human being. When we are freed from seeking the approval of other people, we don't need to be in control because we realize God is in control.

Am I Frequently Nervous, and Does My Nervousness Lead to Demonstrating Nervous Habits?

If we have given ourselves to the Lord completely, what should we be nervous or anxious about? He cares and provides for his children. Hannah Whitall Smith told the story of a man who was laboring down a road and bending under a heavy burden. A wagon rolled alongside the man, and the driver of the wagon kindly offered a ride to the struggling man. The burdened man gladly accepted the offer and took a seat on the back of the wagon.

The driver then glanced back at the man and noticed the traveler still struggling under the burden. Puzzled, the kindhearted driver asked, "Why don't you just lay down the burden?" "Oh," the man replied, "I feel that it is almost too much to ask you to carry me, and I could not think of letting you carry my burden, too."[2]

If God is not carrying your burdens (health, family, house, business, reputation, etc.), he is not carrying all of you. "Do not be anxious about anything, but in everything, by prayer and petition, with thanksgiving, present your requests to God. And the peace of God, which transcends all understanding, will guard your hearts and your minds in Christ Jesus" (Phil. 4:6–7).

Imagine walking into your child's room one evening and noticing a look of bewilderment on her face. You ask your daughter, "What's the matter?" "I'm worried and afraid," is her reply. You probe a little further, "What are you worried about?" She answers, "I'm afraid we won't have anything to eat tomorrow. And I'm scared someone will come and take away our house." The possibility of her fears becoming reality are remote, so as you suppress a smile you reassure her of your commitment and ability to meet all of her needs.

After settling your daughter's fears, you leave her room, wishing every crisis could be solved as easily. You turn out her light and close the door behind you. Then the next night you go through the same drama, and the next and the next. No matter how hard you try to ease her anxiety, your promises to her do not remove her worry. How would you as a parent feel?

You would probably be hurt, and maybe a little angry—not because of her fear but because her anxiety is based on a lack of trust. By her actions, she has told you she doesn't trust you to provide what she needs.

When we worry and become anxious, we essentially tell God, "My circumstances aren't determined and controlled by you but by human beings or by chance. I will do what I can to seek approval from people who can provide my basic needs."

Jesus said, "Therefore I tell you, do not worry about your life, what you will eat or drink; or about your body, what you will wear. Is not life more important than food, and the body more important than clothes? Look at the birds of the air; they do not sow or reap or store away in barns, and yet your heavenly Father feeds them. Are you not much more valuable than they?" (Matt. 6:25–26).

Said the robin to the sparrow:
"I should really like to know

Why these anxious human beings
Rush about and worry so."
Said the sparrow to the robin:
"Friend, I think that it must be
That they have no heavenly Father,
Such as cares for you and me." [3]

An honest self-evaluation here may sting a little. How often do we compromise on a conviction because to stand firm would affect our bank account or our paycheck? Rather than rock the boat, wouldn't letting a matter go be much easier? Sure it would be, but it would also mean giving in to fear of man.

Larry was a friend of mine who worked for a youth counseling organization. His superiors instructed Larry to give the young people he counseled advice contrary to Larry's convictions as a Christian. Larry, his wife Marsha, and their children depended on his income to meet all their financial needs. Larry and Marsha were committed to being obedient to the Lord and trusting him to meet all their needs. Larry tenured his resignation without another job to turn to.

My faith grew as I watched the peace Larry and Marsha experienced because they sought to please God instead of people. Larry shared this pilgrimage with his adult Sunday School class. He didn't tell the story as a burden or a great need, although the need was obvious. He shared the story as a reason to praise the Lord for providing everything they needed.

Many people would have attempted to justify compromise, but not Larry. The results of refusing to give the ungodly counsel were serious, but Larry was faithful and obedient, and God was faithful in return. God gave Larry another job, and although he had to relocate his family, he would do it all over again.

God was glorified in Larry's life, and the contentment his family experienced because of their obedience far outweighed any inconvenience created as a result of their move. "I have not seen the righteous forsaken, Or his descendants begging bread" (Ps. 37:25, NASB). Proverbs 10:3 reads, "The LORD does not let the righteous go hungry, but he thwarts the craving of the wicked."

Do I Exaggerate the Facts or Give Partial Information to Improve My Image?

Another symptom of one who seeks human approval is exaggeration of facts. We tend to exaggerate the truth when the truth by itself is not enough to impress others. Sometimes telling the facts alone will not produce the desired response from a person whom we are trying to impress.

In a discourse on telling the truth, Jesus said, "Simply let your 'Yes' be 'Yes,' and your 'No,' 'No'; anything beyond this comes from the evil one" (Matt. 5:37). Perhaps the truth will not grab a person's attention. The facts alone won't always impress others, but that's OK. Believers are to speak the truth.

The only opinion that should matter to us is the opinion of our heavenly Father, and when you think about it, he is not impressed with statistics—real or exaggerated. God is not impressed with our titles, honors, accomplishments, or possessions. Psalm 50:10–12 reads, "For every animal of the forest is mine, and the cattle on a thousand hills. I know every bird in the mountains, and the creatures of the field are mine . . . For the world is mine, and all that is in it."

The finest aircraft does not impress the One who created the eagle and made it soar. A submarine that carries humans underwater is not impressive to the One who created a fish to carry a prophet in its belly for three days. The most beautiful piece of art isn't impressive to the master-potter who fashioned with his own hands his masterpieces called man and woman.

Babe Ruth supposedly said, "It ain't braggin' if it's true," but the person whose desire is to please the Father does not need to impress anyone else. With regard to *real* achievements, the best policy is to "Let another man praise you, and not your own mouth" (Prov. 27:2). I recently had an experience that put this principle in perspective for me again. I am periodically asked by friends, colleagues, and students to allow them to use me as a reference on a résumé or as a character reference for an international study program offered by Mississippi College. I consider being asked an honor. I confess it does wonders for the old ego to discover someone believes your recommendation may help them out. Sometimes people have even gotten accepted in spite of including my name as a reference.

The other day I received a reality check when I was asked by a friend to allow him to use my name as a reference. Nothing unusual about that. *Glad to oblige*, I thought. Then I asked, "A reference for what?" I was not expecting the answer my friend gave. There is no way I can convey my feelings when he told me the reason he wanted to use my name.

He told me he and his wife were on a waiting list for an adoption. It's not what you might think, however. This couple wanted to adopt a registered Rhodesian Ridgeback.

The Ridgeback is a large dog with short red hair, a portion of which stands up on its back. They are highly popular to potential owners for property protection because they appear aggressive due to the hair standing up on their back, but they are docile around children and guests to the home. Their popularity has resulted in a seller's market, and there is a waiting list to adopt these animals.

So now I know I have arrived. This is what it's all about: the education, the experience, the network of friends and colleagues, the prestige of a University Chair, and the privilege of being used as a reference for a dog. Talk about putting things in perspective. I asked just one favor from my friend (yes, I still consider him a friend) who made the request: *Please Don't Tell Anyone!* But now I guess I've told everyone, haven't I?

My point is, don't take yourself too seriously. God is not impressed with our best efforts if we aren't motivated out of our love for him, even if you work "like a dog" (sorry, I couldn't resist that). Remember Paul's words, "For by the grace given me I say to every one of you: Do not think of yourself more highly than you ought, but rather think of yourself with sober judgment, in accordance with the measure of faith God has given you" (Rom. 12:3).

Exaggeration is not the only way we deceive people to improve their opinion of us. Sometime we give only partial information so people will think more highly of us than they might if they knew the absolute truth. I heard of two pastors who saw one another at a pastor's conference after not seeing one another for several years.

The first pastor asked his friend, "How many are you all running in worship now?" Unnecessarily embarrassed by the truth, the second man answered, "Oh, between four and five hundred." The truth was they were averaging about sixty-five in worship, which the second man rationalized as being between four and five hundred.

In the above scenario, a half-truth was a whole lie. Proverbs 12:13 reads, "An evil man is trapped by his sinful talk, but a righteous man escapes trouble." A few verses later the author added, "The LORD detests lying lips, but he delights in men who are truthful" (Prov. 12:22). Proverbs 8:13 reads, "To fear the LORD is to hate evil; I hate pride and arrogance, evil behavior and perverse speech." Of the seven items that are detestable to the Lord listed in Proverbs 6, the first two are haughty eyes and a *lying tongue*.

A person whose desire is to please his or her heavenly Father has no reason to exaggerate or to tell half-truths. Since our desire is to be obedient to God, the wisest approach is to let the truth speak for itself.

Do I Drop Names So Others Will Be Impressed?

Can't you tell when someone is trying to impress you by reporting on celebrities they have met, or important functions they have attended, or the people present at their last "power lunch"? Certainly you can, and most people can see through our attempts to impress them by name-dropping too.

Friends and acquaintances add so much to life. One of the joys of being a Christian is experiencing relationships with brothers and sisters in Christ whom we would not know outside of the body of Christ, but knowing God as our friend is far more important than having "important" friends here on earth.

Volumes have been written and entire series of sermons have been preached about the faith of Abraham. Of all the designations of the father of our faith, the most prestigious description of him in the Bible is "friend God" (2 Chron. 20:7). What an epitaph! Now there is a name to drop.

Can't you imagine Abraham's conversation with the clan leaders? "Abraham, have you met with anyone important lately?" "Well, this morning I had a special time with my heavenly Father. He's such a faithful friend." "Abraham, who are you keeping company with these days?" "The other evening, I walked along the river bank with the Lord. I've never felt closer to him."

Folks, I'm telling you, if you and I can lay our heads down on our pillows at night and know that we have a friend in God and that he will be ready the next day to pick up where we left off, we are blessed beyond measure. What's really important is not that you are able to call "important," famous, or influential people in this world your friends, but that the One who really matters knows you as *his* friend.

At the memorial service for legendary baseball great Mickie Mantle, Bobby Thompson, Mick's friend and former teammate, shared his conversations with Mantle that occurred shortly before the death of the lovable country boy from Oklahoma. Mickey was uncomfortable with being considered a role model.

35

His personal struggles with alcohol were matters of public record.

Mick knew his life was drawing short, so he requested the companionship of his friend Bobby Thompson. Thompson is also a minister of the gospel and a popular Christian speaker. Mantle leaned on him for spiritual counsel toward the end of his life.

In his concluding comments at the memorial service, Bobby shared the victory Mantle experienced when he confessed his sins to Jesus Christ and received God's loving forgiveness and hope of eternal life. I'll never forget Thompson's closing remarks concerning the measure of a person's significance.

With confidence in his voice, Thompson placed more importance on Mickey's name (or any other name for that matter) being written in the record books of heaven than on the record books of earth. He closed with the following poem:

Your name may not appear down here
in this world's hall of fame.
In fact you may be so unknown that
no one knows your name.
The trophies, the honors, the flash bulbs here
may pass you by and neon lights ablue.
But if you love and serve the Lord,
then I have news for you.
This hall of fame is only good as
long as time shall be,
But keep in mind God's hall of fame is for eternity.
This crowd on earth they soon
forget the heroes of the past.
They cheer like mad until you fall
and that's how long you last.
But in God's hall of fame,
By just believing in his Son, inscribed
you'll find your name.

I tell you friend I wouldn't trade my name
however small,
That's written there beyond the stars
in that celestial hall,
For every famous name on Earth
or glory that they share.
I'd rather be an unknown and have
my name up there.[4]

No matter how many people know your name, I hope your name is written on the record books of heaven as well.

Do I Have Trouble Being Transparent and Honest with People about My Weaknesses, Fearing They Will Think Less of Me If They Know the Truth about Me?

For most people, sharing weaknesses, shortcomings, and character flaws doesn't come easily. May I share a secret with you? Most people who know you already know your weaknesses and shortcomings as well as your strengths. When we become transparent and honest about our shortcomings, we begin the process of being forgiven and healed. "Therefore confess your sins to each other and pray for each other so that you may be healed" (James 5:16).

When we honestly confess and admit our sins and weaknesses to a trusted friend, an unbelievable burden is lifted from our shoulders. But trusting someone at that level involves risk.

Instead of seeking the counsel and encouragement of others, however, we try to deal with our weaknesses in other ways. For example, we may cover up our sin or character flaw—just pretend that the weakness doesn't exist. This leads to more guilt and frustration. "He who conceals his sins does not prosper, but whoever confesses and renounces them finds mercy" (Prov. 28:13).

Another means of dealing with our faults is to do something to make up for the sin. For example, instead of dealing directly with the sin, it's easier to give a huge gift to the church or perform some service to the community.

The only permanent, satisfying way to deal with sin is to do it God's way. Admit it (that's confession), and quit it (that's repentance). And part of admitting the fault is finding a *trusted* brother or sister in Christ in whom we can confide. A major difficulty in confessing to another person is not that we have no one in whom we can confide, but that we are too proud to be honest. Our problem is pride. We care more about what others think of us than dealing with our sin God's way and being cleansed.

Remember, others have no reason to look down their noses at you. They have their own problems. When we can swallow our pride and say, "You know, if I'm honest, I'm taking a risk that someone's opinion of me might go down. But I care more about pleasing God than someone else. And I know God is pleased with a humble heart. I'm going to swallow my pride and trust the Lord for my reputation." "When pride comes, then comes disgrace, but with humility comes wisdom" (Prov. 11:2).

Regarding being honest with others about our faults, please let me leave you with one final word. When you are honest about your weaknesses, most people will not think less of you. In most cases, your stock will go up. But even if someone takes advantage of your vulnerability, rest assured that God will honor your obedience. And his opinion is the only one that really matters.

Are My Feelings Easily Hurt?

Have you noticed how people have to walk on eggshells these days for fear they will offend an individual or group by what they say? People have gotten so sensitive lately. It seems like you can't open your mouth without offending someone.

For example, the American Kennel Club recently recalled the latest edition of The Complete Dog Book, a guide for dog owners and breeders. Some pet owners became angry at the AKC because some of the nation's most popular breeds were listed in the book as "not good with children."

Now I understand the indignation, especially considering the important implications for the safety of children. But some of the responses by dog owners and breeders bordered on the ridiculous. I heard one irate pet owner say, "This is nothing but pure racism! Canine racism!" Don't you think that's carrying it a little too far? The AKC did print an apology: "The AKC sincerely regrets the distress caused to dog owners and breeders by the errors. AKC neither agrees with nor endorses the material."

In another incident, an article in USA Today described a parody that circulated on the Internet that changed The Twelve Days of Christmas into "'the Eurocentrically imposed mid-winter festival' on which 'my significant other in a consenting adult, monogamous relationship gave to me' gifts that include 'eight economically disadvantaged female persons stealing milk products from enslaved Bovine-Americans' and 'seven endangered swans swimming on federally protected wetlands.'"[5]

I hope you're smiling at the above cases, but if we Christians are going to be salt and light in our communities, we must have tough skins and a soft heart, not vice versa. Let's try not to get our feelings hurt so easily.

Now I know we all learn a little rhyme when we're young that goes like this:

Sticks and stones may break my bones,
But words will never hurt me.

When we said that rhyme as children, some of us weren't being completely honest. We knew then and we know now—words *do* hurt. We could change the rhyme to read something like this:

Sticks and stones may break my bones,
But they may soon be mended.
Names and words may hurt my feelings,
And the damage never ended.

Too much concern about the sensitivity of people also causes Christians to not speak out about important moral issues. Those who are speaking out and seeking the approval of God instead of people are paying a price for their courage.

Reggie White is arguably one of the most popular players in the National Football League. He's known as the "Minister of Defense" to his fans and teammates, partly because of his status as an all-pro defensive lineman and partly because he is a pastor of a church in Tennessee.

As one of the most popular public figures in the state of Wisconsin, White was invited recently to speak to the Wisconsin state legislature. He gladly accepted. But his address was unique.

Normally, when someone is asked to address the body of government officials, the person makes some polite comments, adds five to ten minutes of fluff, and steps away from the microphone. Not Reggie.

Reggie White talked about things like sin and the need for our society to turn our hearts back to God and to seek him for the answers to the problems in our nation. In his speech, although affirming God's love for all people, White called the practice of homosexual behavior a sin. That was all it took for Reggie to be accused of spreading "divisiveness and bigotry." CBS officials, who had planned on White joining them in the announcers' booth after his retirement, canceled plans to offer him a contract.

Never mind that Reggie White had founded the organization Urban Hope to support inner-city business training and investment or that he sacrificially gives of his time to talk to teens and young people about the dangers of illegal drugs, alcohol abuse, and gang violence.

Reggie was tried and found guilty in the court of public opinion because he dared stand on the teachings of Scripture concerning ungodly behavior. His response was classic: "I didn't start a ministry to please everybody." Concerning the decision by CBS officials, he added, "I like people to think good of me, but I'm not going to sell out."[6] Thanks, Reggie. We need real heroes like you.

Sometimes people may intentionally say or do things that offend you. On some occasions, people will offend you unintentionally. When this occurs, remember, you're self-worth is not based on their opinion of you. No one can *make* you have a bad day or be discouraged. Those are conditions we choose by how we react to others. When someone hurts you, intentionally or unintentionally, take your ears off of them and tune in to the voice of the Lord. When we seek his pleasure, the words of others don't carry near as much weight.

Do I Have Difficulty Serving Others?

I think one reason I admire people who possess the heart of a servant is because service is difficult for me. That may sound odd coming from someone who spent ten years serving others in the ministry as an undershepherd, but it's the truth. I am ashamed to admit how many times I served others out of a sense of duty and obligation (not *always* a bad reason I might add), instead of being motivated by compassion for others.

Often I did, and still do, visit the hurting or grieving because I love them and because that's what Jesus would do. But there were nights when I was exhausted and hadn't seen my family all day, and my heart was not into going by the funeral home to minister to a grieving family. On those days, I went because I didn't want people to think they had a lazy or uncaring pastor.

I wish my motives would have been more pure all of the time. Maybe you have never served mainly because others expected you to, but sometimes that's what motivated me. Not very admirable, huh? So when I see someone who has dedicated his or her life not just to serve, but to be a servant—continually, deliberately, consistently—I stand and applaud. That takes courage. That takes someone who says, "I don't care if others take advantage of me, or question my motives, or treat me like a doormat, or don't say thank you, or don't even know my name—I'm going to be a servant to others."

Service was Jesus' whole reason for coming to earth: "For even the Son of Man did not come to be served, but to serve, and to give his life as a ransom for many" (Mark 10:45).

I don't understand all the irony of service, but inevitably the servant's position is one of strength, not weakness. This reality makes some people uneasy about allowing others to serve them. When the servant expects nothing in return, the one being served feels uncomfortable. I'm not sure which is easier, being an obedient servant or being a gracious recipient of service.

I will never forget attending the Promise Keepers Clergy Conference in Atlanta, Georgia, during the peak of the PK movement. The conference took place just after the "Million Man March," organized by the Nation of Islam leader Louis Farrakhan. Tony Evans, pastor and author was a speaker for the PK conference as was Wellington Boone, another favorite speaker and author of those attending the conferences. Both men happen to be African-Americans.

Tony Evans had come under criticism by some in the African-American community because he chose not to participate in nor promote the Million Man March. Here is a man who had worked virtually his entire adult life to proclaim the gospel message to all people no matter the color of their skin. He had been bold and proactive in trying to reconcile people of different skin colors.

Tony's motive was not to attract the public spotlight, but to share the love and forgiveness he had experienced as a child of God. He believes we as the body of Christ can see many of our nation's woes cured as hearts are changed by the good news of Jesus' love for us. In Tony's words, "We may have come over here on different ships, but we're in the same boat now."

I've never been quite the same since that conference in Atlanta, partly because of an act of service by Wellington Boone intended to affirm his brother, Tony Evans. Right in the middle of Boone's message, he looked back at Evans, who was seated on the platform with several others.

Then in front of over 50,000 ministers Wellington said something like this: "Brother, I want to affirm you for the stand you have taken. I know that you have had to stand alone on many occasions, and I'm asking you to forgive me for allowing that to happen. I look up to you and respect you for your courage. I pledge right now to stand with you and work with you. I just want to serve you, my brother."

Then it got really good. Boone said, "If I had some water I would wash your feet right now to show you I'm ready to serve you." He shouldn't have said that unless he was ready to do it. With all the testosterone in that place, combined with the spiritual intensity of the occasion, you could have cut the atmosphere with a knife.

When Boone made his statement to Evans, a lone Caucasian man in a baseball cap came running up to the platform carrying a bottle of drinking water and waving a towel. He placed the water and towel on the stage in front of Boone's feet. He was followed by another man who did the same, then another. Finally, Boone said, "You white brothers are crazy." By this time, most present were laughing and crying at the same time.

Someone on the stage placed a chair behind Boone. Tony Evans, though reluctantly at first, was led by the men sitting beside him to sit in the chair. Boone slipped off the shoes of Evans and began to wash his feet and encourage him with more affirming words. Tony Evans wept.

I'll never forget that day. I saw demonstrated something I knew to be true: in order for a person to humble himself or herself and become a genuine servant, he or she must care more about obeying and honoring God than about appearing "dignified" before people.

Here's where the irony comes in. Not only was Evans, a Christian brother, lifted up and encouraged, but Boone's stock went up as well. Those men attending the conference respected him even more after he voluntarily took on the role of a servant. But if you care more about appearing dignified before people than following Christ's example of servanthood, you will never know the joy that comes with true humility.

Do I Have Difficulty Allowing Others to Serve Me?

Would you have allowed someone to wash your feet in front of 50,000 other people? For that matter, would you allow another person to extend an act of service toward you in the presence of one other person? Most people feel awkward when someone else shows them an act of service. We become uneasy, at least in part, because of our pride.

Simon Peter refused to allow Jesus to wash his feet. The Lord said to Peter, "If I do not wash you, you have no part with Me" (John 13:8, NASB).

I wish I could say I am a gracious receiver of service. I am not. It's hard for me to accept genuine acts of service from others. While my family and I were in seminary, we struggled financially just like everyone else we knew in school. Don't get me wrong—we had all our financial *needs* met. We were serving a small church family who provided for our needs, but traveling to and from New Orleans every week and caring for two young children stretched our tiny budget like crepe paper at a high school reunion.

From paycheck to paycheck, things were pretty tight, but compared to some of my classmates, we were rich. For example, my brother-in-law, Chip, and his roommate were not serving in a full-time staff position and still had the expenses of living and going to school. Their budget was so lean, they kept a jar of peanut butter and a loaf of bread handy all the time.

Chip and Jeff were blessed however, because Chip's sister, my wife Page, is absolutely the most thoughtful, generous person I know. We didn't have an abundance, but what we had she was always willing to share. And share we did. Many afternoons

Chip and Jeff would put their legs under our table and enjoy God's blessing just like the rest of us. After all, it all belongs to the Lord anyway.

The afternoon of my birthday, after we finished our meal, we sat around and talked, like we normally did after lunch. Then Chip handed me an envelope and said, "Happy Birthday." Now Chip was a generous guy and all, but we weren't in the habit of exchanging birthday cards. After all, he *is* my brother-in-law.

I was moved by the gesture, but after I opened the card I was shocked when two crisp twenty-dollar bills fell into my lap. Forty bucks!! That was a long time ago—two children and a mortgage ago to be exact. Forty dollars went a long way!

I didn't have time to think long before I said, "Chip, I can't take this money from you. I know you don't have *four* dollars to give away, much less forty."

Then Chip explained, "Les, Jeff and I really appreciate you, Page, and the boys opening up your home to us. We know you all don't have a lot, but you've always shared what you have with us. You're right, I don't have forty dollars, but I began to pray that God would give me forty dollars to help replenish a little of what Jeff and I have eaten.

"The other day, a man came up to me at church [Chip was serving as an intern], and as he was shaking my hand, he put these two twenties in my palm. The man said, 'Chip, I don't know why, but I really feel like the Lord wants me to give you this. I guess you know what it's for.'" Then Chip looked at me and said, "Les, I can't keep the money. It isn't mine. God gave it to me to give to you."

For a moment I was speechless. Then I said, "Well, Chip, why did you just ask for forty bucks? Next time ask for at least a hundred!"

Since then, I've wondered why I was so reluctant to take the money from Chip before I knew the specifics. I believe it was probably because of my pride. At times like that I can almost hear myself say, "Lord, you're not going to wash my feet."

In order to receive service we have to acknowledge our need. When we serve we meet the needs of others. When others serve you, they meet needs you have. Most of us don't want to admit dependence upon someone else. That's why I had difficulty accepting the gift from Chip.

If I had refused to receive his gift, I would have deprived him of the joy of obedience to God and service to his Christian brother. I would have been standing in the way of God's channel of blessing for me and my family.

Thanks, Chip—not only for your obedience and willingness to serve another, but for reminding me of my own pride and my need for the service of others. After all, we are always dependent upon God for everything. You may have a million dollars in the bank, but it can be gone in one moment.

No matter how much or how little you have, it's a good day when you acknowledge that every good and perfect gift comes from our Heavenly Father. The psalmist wrote, "I was young and now I am old, yet I have never seen the righteous forsaken or their children begging bread" (Ps. 37:25).

Being a generous giver and an obedient servant are admirable traits, but the next time someone wants to serve you, be a gracious receiver. You probably need what is being offered, and the other person needs to practice his or her service.

Summary

If any or all of these symptoms apply to you, don't deny it. Instead, be thankful to the Lord for revealing them to you. Now you can begin the process of being freed from the burden of pleasing others. Since God is able to do exceedingly, abundantly above all that we can ask or imagine, he can certainly liberate us from this condition.

Now that we've identified some symptoms of seeking the approval of people, let's see some of the consequences of seeking to please others instead of God.

Prayer

Holy Father, I desire your pleasure more than anything. You and you alone are worthy of my adoration. I now realize there have been times when I've given my allegiance to others. Thank you for your loving probe into my life. It isn't pleasant for me, but I know it's what I need.

I have a long way to go. How can I overcome being preoccupied with the opinions of others? I know your opinion of me is the only one that matters.

Please give me the wisdom and grace I need for this journey. I'll trust you to see me through and show me in your Word the course to take.

Chapter 4
Living to Please Others

Hear me, you who know what is right, you people who have
my law in your hearts: Do not fear the reproach of men or
be terrified by their insults.
(Isa. 51:7)

Do not be afraid of those who kill the body but cannot kill
the soul. Rather, be afraid of the One who can destroy both
soul and body in hell. (Matt. 10:28)

The results of living to please people can be devastating.
These consequences range from minor results to matters of eternal life and death and affect Christians as well as unbelievers.
Although all of these consequences can have serious implications, some lead to more costly results than others. As we examine some of the consequences of yielding to the fear of man,
we'll begin with the less serious and move to the more costly.

Bondage under the Opinions of Others

Living to please others can place shackles on the one who
gives in to it. That's what the writer of the proverb meant when
he wrote, "Fear of man will prove to be a snare, but whoever
trusts in the LORD is kept safe" (Prov. 29:25).

The Hebrew word for snare or net is resheth. The use of
this term denotes a bird being caught in a net, unable to perform what God created it to do—to soar in the heavens. Picture a grand eagle flopping under a net canopy, helpless and

vulnerable to an approaching predator. As sad an image as that is, even more tragic is a child of God flopping under the net of the fear of man.

God created you to know him and to glorify him with your life. Glorifying God requires taking risks, but sometimes you have to go out on a limb—that's where the fruit is. For example, Moses allowed himself to be bound by his fear of man for forty years. After killing an Egyptian taskmaster for mistreating a Hebrew slave, he feared Pharaoh would discover his deed, so Moses fled Egypt. He settled in Midian and tended sheep for Jethro, his father-in-law.

After forty years of tending sheep in obscurity, Moses encountered the living God. Moses was so filled with fear at that burning bush experience, he hid his face (Exod. 3:6). Moses took a big step in overcoming his fear of man on that day. He descended the mountain to stand before Pharaoh and to command him to let God's people go.

For Moses, overcoming fear of man meant the literal liberation of God's people in physical bondage. God's purpose for the Israelites included preparing the world for the coming of his Son, the anointed one, but Pharaoh had thrown a net over God's people, and he didn't give up his hold on them easily.

Finally, Pharaoh let the people go. The net was cut, and the people flew. Although their flight included an air pocket now and then, and some turbulence occasionally, they finally reached the promised land, and God was glorified in their victory. He even reminded them, "You yourselves have seen what I did to Egypt, and how I carried you on eagles' wings and brought you to myself" (Exod. 19:4).

Our bondage may not occur in Egypt. We may not be bound by literal chains. But we do have different kinds of bondage that confine us. We will never be who God created us to be while we are caught in the snare of the fear of man. Whether in your home, or school, or business, or church, God uses people who take risks for him.

John Hyde is one of my best friends in the world. He constantly serves as an encourager to me. John overcame incredible odds and glorified the Lord in the process. When we were juniors in high school, John was in a near fatal automobile crash that put him in a coma for three months. When he came out of the coma, he couldn't speak, he couldn't walk, and he had lost mobility in most of his body. John was glad to be alive and determined to begin a long process of rehabilitation. He was determined to trust God for his recovery and not fear obstacles he knew God could get him through.

John wanted to exercise his mind and his spirit, and at the same time use his circumstances as a chance to share the power of God to others. He believed one way to accomplish all the above was to memorize Scripture, but since he couldn't speak or write legibly he needed a way to express himself. His family gave him a child's small alphabet board with magnetic letters. John would point to each letter, one by one, to spell out each word of his memory verses. Even retelling this story makes me emotional as I see John lying in that nursing home bed showing more courage and determination than many people who live in much more desirable circumstances.

I remember visiting John after he memorized his first verse after awakening from the coma. Everyone in the room with John shared his sense of accomplishment as he pointed out the letters to Isaiah 40:31: "But those who hope in the LORD will renew their strength. They will *soar on wings like eagles*; they will run and not grow weary, They will walk and not be faint" (emphasis mine).

John still gets around by way of a wheelchair, but he is not in bondage. His courage and faith have set him free. He has earned a seminary degree, and shares what God is doing in his life whenever he has the opportunity. But here is what I wanted you to see through John's experience: when you give in to fear and refuse to trust in God, you have fallen into Satan's snare and you will not soar. God wants to liberate you through your faith in him so that you can mount up with wings as an eagle and fly. "My eyes are ever on the LORD, for only he will release my feet from the snare" (Ps. 25:15).

Frustration and Discontentment

A true child of God will be satisfied only when pleasing his or her heavenly Father. We may try to substitute other people or things in God's place, but ultimately those alternatives will not satisfy or give the child of God a sense of contentment.

Feelings of discontentment and dissatisfaction can cause one to become short, defensive, and grouchy toward others, even toward loved ones such as a spouse or child. The scenario is commonplace. A person is more concerned about his reputation, or her bank account, or what kind of car he drives than about being obedient to his or her heavenly Father.

Since only God can satisfy the inner needs of human beings, our hearts are restless without his blessing. Augustine wrote, "Thou hast made us for Thyself, and our hearts are restless until they find their rest in Thee."

Paul advised his Philippian readers to have an attitude of thanks in all things instead of possessing a heart of discontentment. The person who has learned the secret of contentment is blessed by the Father with peace. "Do not be anxious about anything, but in everything, by prayer and petition, with thanksgiving, present your requests to God. And the peace of God, which transcends all understanding, will guard your hearts and your minds in Christ Jesus" (Phil. 4:6–7).

Lack of Joy

One of the greatest blessings you and I have as children of God is the joy he provides when we serve him and others. But the person who does good primarily to impress others robs herself of a unique, God-given joy. In the Sermon on the Mount, Jesus mentioned three common expressions of faith: prayer, giving to the needy, and fasting. These were basic expressions of

Jewish religion in the first century. Jesus assumed they would be performed. He didn't say "*If* you give, fast, and pray," but "*When*" you practice these spiritual disciplines, do it in the following way (see Matt. 6:1–18).

Evidently, some were practicing these spiritual disciplines in order to gain the approval of others and not out of obedience to the Father. Jesus described both the unacceptable way to perform these duties and the acceptable way to practice them. He instructed his audience, whether their expression of faith was giving to the needy, praying, or fasting, to do the deed in secret. Then God would see and he would reward them, and when God gives a reward, he does a thorough job. John Stott wrote,

> The contrast is not between a secret gift and a public reward, but between the men who neither see nor reward the gift and the God who does both. . . .
>
> What, then, is the "reward" which the heavenly Father gives the secret giver? It is neither public nor necessarily future. It is probably the only reward which genuine love wants when making a gift to the needy, namely to see the need relieved. When through his gifts the hungry are fed, the naked clothed, the sick healed, the oppressed freed and the lost saved, the love which prompted the gift is satisfied. Such love (which is God's own love expressed through man) brings with it its own secret joys, and desires no other reward.
>
> To sum up, our Christian giving is to be neither before men (waiting for the clapping to begin), nor even before ourselves (our left hand applauding our right hand's generosity) but "before God," who sees our secret heart and rewards us with the discovery that, as Jesus said, "It is more blessed to give than to receive."[1]

In other words, no human being can supply the utter joy one experiences by serving the Lord with pure motives. God applauds genuine service. Wouldn't you like to hear that kind of heavenly ovation?

Stifling of the Gospel

One of the most serious results of a displaced approval drive is the hindrance of the spread of the good news about Jesus. In the first century, the early Christians told others about Christ with boldness, even when their boldness led to death, as in the case of Stephen (Acts 7).

We'll deal later with the affects of people-pleasing on evangelism, but think about this for a moment. Imagine what our world would be like if those early followers of Christ had been timid about their faith in Jesus. Jesus has had an impact on millions of individuals and many of our institutions.

Think of the changed lives, the Church, hospitals, universities such as Harvard and Princeton, which were established primarily for the training of ministers—these have been impacted by people who were bold enough to say, "Whether it is right in the sight of God to give heed to you rather than to God, you be the judge; for we cannot stop speaking what we have seen and heard" (Acts 4:19–20).

Because of their boldness, the good news about Jesus was not stamped out by the Roman emperors or the religious authorities, but was proclaimed unashamedly and without hindrance (Acts 28:31).

Divine Discipline

If you belong to God—if you are his son or daughter, he will not ignore your disobedience forever. I wish I knew a gentler way to say that, but I don't. Sooner or later, if you really belong to the Father and you disobey him, he will discipline you. When that happens, it won't be pleasant. But remember, his discipline is always remedial. God's discipline is intended to bring you back to him and to protect you as his child. The author of Hebrews wrote, "The Lord disciplines those he loves, . . . but God disciplines us for our good, that we may share in his holiness" (Heb. 12:6a, 10b).

The story of a prophet who learned this principle the hard way is recorded in the Old Testament book of Jonah. This wayward preacher was instructed to go to the wicked city of Ninevah. Jonah feared the reaction of the Ninevites to his preaching, more than the reaction of God to his disobedience. God told him to go east, but Jonah headed west across the Mediterranean Sea. Even in Jonah's disobedience, God loved him too much to let him go. Make no mistake, God could have tapped another person on the shoulder and written Jonah off, but instead he chose to pursue the prodigal and provide the means to bring him back.

I love the way the author of the book relates God's sovereign activity in the life of this runaway. First the Lord sent a violent storm on the sea to alarm the sailors into waking Jonah who was snuggled below the deck. Jonah fessed up that he was running away from the Lord and convinced the men their only hope of being saved from the storm was to throw him overboard. They reluctantly followed his advice.

God then provided his own submarine in the form of a great fish, which carried its passenger for three days. Finally, the prophet repented and vowed to God he would go to the Ninevites and trust God for the results.

Much to Jonah's amazement the Ninevites actually listened to God's instructions, repented of their wickedness, and humbled themselves before the Lord. God had compassion on the people of Ninevah, and, instead of pouring out his wrath, he poured out his grace and mercy.

Jonah became angry when God spared the Ninevites, and he went out east of the city. He told God to go ahead and end his life right then and there. After building a shelter for himself, Jonah sat under it and pouted.

Fortunately for Jonah, God showed the same patience for the prophet as he had the prophet's enemies. God provided a vine that grew quickly over the shelter and gave shade to the prophet. The shade from the vine pleased Jonah, but the next day God provided a worm that chewed the vine and caused it to wither and die.

That afternoon was a real scorcher. Jonah missed the shade of his little vine. He was discouraged and confused over God's sparing the Ninevites. Jonah was having a tough time. Again he addressed the Lord: "It would be better for me to die than to live."

After letting Jonah have his say, God finally sat him down and gave him the reprimand he deserved. God said, "Jonah, you are showing a great deal of concern over this vine, which you had nothing to do with creating. You didn't tend it, and you didn't make it grow. It sprang up overnight, and it died overnight. Ninevah has more than 120,000 people who can't tell their right hand from their left. I *did* create them. They belong to me. You may not be concerned about them, but I am. I'm going to show them the same grace I showed you."

Jonah's story is a wonderful lesson about God's relentless grace toward two groups who didn't deserve it—one thought he did, the others knew they didn't. But what I want to point out to you is this: the events most of us would consider curses in the life of Jonah were actually blessings provided by God.

Most people wouldn't consider a catastrophic storm, a smelly fish with a huge appetite, and a plant-eating worm as blessings from the Lord, but these were. God strategically placed them in the life of Jonah. The results were that the Ninevites were spared, and the prophet got a much-needed lesson in Grace 101.

Is there a circumstance in your life that you consider a curse or a burden right now? I don't know what's behind it, but could it be that God is *providing* the difficulty so you will be obedient and turn to Him? If you are his child and your concern over what others think causes you to ignore his voice, he will discipline you. He loves you too much not to.

When God provides a storm, or a fish, or a worm in your life, figuratively or literally, remember his discipline is remedial. David wrote, "Surely goodness and mercy shall follow me all the days of my life" (Ps. 23:6, KJV). The word for *follow* in the twenty-third Psalm means "to pursue." That's why Francis Thompson called God the Hound of Heaven. Remember, God is more concerned with your character than with your comfort.

When God shows us his tough love, and the result is our repentance and obedience, others hear the Good News about Jesus in our words or by our actions or both. That's what having a testimony is all about. Yet even when others see what God has done in your life, their concern over what others think of them may cause them to reject the Good News of God's grace through Jesus Christ. This rejection of God's love leads to the last and most serious consequence.

Eternal Separation from God

The results of pleasing people rather than God that we've discussed so far are tragic, but this result has the most severe eternal consequences. If concern over what others think leads to rejection of Jesus as Lord, the inevitable result is hell. Jesus took this matter so seriously that he spoke in simple, straightforward language concerning choosing to seek human approval rather than God's: "Do not be afraid of those who kill the body but cannot kill the soul. Rather, be afraid of the One who can destroy both soul and body in hell. . . . Whoever acknowledges me before men, I will also acknowledge him before my Father in heaven. But whoever disowns me before men, I will disown him before my Father in heaven" (Matt. 10:28, 32–33).

Jesus told a parable about a certain rich man whose land was productive beyond his expectations. Unprepared to store the abundant harvest, the man decided to build bigger barns. But in his obsession to make provisions for his material prosperity, he neglected to plan for his eternal destiny—not a wise move. God said to the man, "You fool! This very night your life will be demanded from you. Then who will get what you have prepared for yourself?" (Luke 12:20).

Dear one, this result alone is sufficient reason for turning from the practice of pleasing others. Flee from it. Repent of it. Don't trust anyone but God with your eternal destiny. I'm not trying to be dramatic. I'm just telling you the truth. When you trust him, he is faithful to deliver you from eternity in the place

Jesus called hell. I realize this isn't a popular subject to talk about (it's not one of my favorite topics to write about either), but the reality of hell is *the* most serious matter regarding the fear of man.

Two verses from Proverbs summarize this principle: "There is a way that seems right to a man, but in the end it leads to death" (Prov. 14:12); and "The fear of the LORD is a fountain of life, turning a man from the snares of death" (Prov. 14:27).

John Avant, pastor of New Hope Baptist Church in Fayetteville, Georgia, tells a story about a man who was knocked unconscious in a car wreck. When he woke up he was screaming violently. After being rushed by ambulance to the hospital, the man discovered he had only a minor concussion. The hospital personnel then asked the man, "Why did you act so violently out there at the accident site?"

The battered man explained, "When I woke up there were people standing all around me, and I saw a word." "A word?" they asked. "Yes," said the man. Then he told them the word and they understood. You see, the wreck took place at a Shell service station, and one of the individuals standing over him was covering up the letter *S* on the Shell sign with his head. Get the picture?

The story may make us smile a bit, but what's tragic is that in addition to some people spending eternity in hell, scores of others are living in a hell of their own making here on earth by seeking the approval of people instead of God.

Summary

The consequences of seeking human approval are severe and numerous. But God wants his children to experience his blessings by overcoming the fear of man and seeking his approval only. Many of these negative consequences of the fear of man have parallel positive results for those who resist the temptation to seek human applause. The rewards of seeking God's approval will be discussed in a later chapter.

Before examining the benefits that will be enjoyed by those who win a victory over their concern for what people think, let's look at some of the qualities that receive the favor of God. These characteristics were demonstrated in the life of Christ and should be apparent in the lives of all of God's offspring.

Prayer

Holy Father, you don't need to be informed about the results of yielding to the fear of man in my life. I've been affected by almost all of them. How many experiences have I missed because I was caught in a snare on the ground instead of soaring in the heavens above?

Forgive me, Lord, for being like the Nazarenes of the first century who didn't see much of your might because of their lack of faith. But thank you for being a God of the second chance, and the third, and the fourth. Thank you for your forgiveness and for your promises of liberation.

Encourage those who are ensnared right now. Liberate them, Lord, by cutting the ropes of Satan's snare so they might mount up with wings as eagles and fly.

Chapter 5
God's Approval Brings Blessing

Be diligent to present yourself approved to God as a
workman who does not need to be ashamed, handling
accurately the word of truth. (2 Tim. 2:15, NASB)

. . . And your Father, who sees what is done in secret, will
reward you. (Matt. 6:18b)

I've lost track of how many times I've told my children, but I guarantee you they never tire of hearing me say it: "No matter what you do, no matter where you go, no matter what happens in the future, I will always love you, and you will always be my son [or daughter, depending on the child]." The children whom the Lord has entrusted to Page and me may have periodic anxiety and stress. They may have some feelings of insecurity, but these feelings should never be the result of doubting whether their mother and I love them.

We try to inform them and demonstrate to them constantly our unconditional love for them. They cannot do anything to earn our love. We love them because we love them. We love them when they obey and when they disobey.

We love them when they spill red Kool-aid on the carpet. We love them when they get sick all over the interior of the van. We love them when they strike out. We love them when they get up on the wrong side of the bed. And we even love them when they tell us "I don't like you." But (you knew there was a catch, didn't you?) their actions and attitudes have a direct result on whether they receive blessings or conflict from us.

God's love for us is never in doubt. He demonstrated his love for us by giving his only Son as a ransom for our sins. He was under no obligation to give us such a demonstration of his love, but he did. And he certainly is not obligated to prove his love continually for you and me, although he does constantly.

Paul hit the nail on the head when he wrote, "You see, at just the right time, when we were still powerless, Christ died for the ungodly. Very rarely will anyone die for a righteous man, though for a good man someone might possibly dare to die. But God demonstrates his own love for us in this: While we were still sinners, Christ died for us," (Rom. 5:6–8). That kind of sacrificial love speaks for itself. That's grace.

God's grace is not determined by our actions or by whether we deserve it. God blesses us with his grace because he wants to. But our actions and attitudes in part determine whether we will experience God's favor and blessings expressed in other ways. Will we experience his blessing as a result of his approval? Or will we experience conflict as a result of his disapproval?

The seed of this idea was planted in my mind during my study on the Beatitudes in Jesus' Sermon on the Mount.[1] In this masterpiece discourse, Jesus described raising the standard in specific areas of our behavior and our attitudes. He instructed his listeners not to have the standards of human beings as their goal, but the standards of God. John Stott called this raising of the standard the "Christian counter-culture."

Let's go back to the example of Jesus telling his listeners to raise the standard in their expressions of their religion, such as giving, prayer, and fasting. He said "Be careful not to do your 'acts of righteousness' *before men*, to be seen by them. If you do, you will have no reward from your Father in heaven. So when you give to the needy, *do not announce it with trumpets*, as the hypocrites do in the synagogues and on the streets, to be honored by men. I tell you the truth, they have received their reward in full" (Matt. 6:1–2, emphases mine).

That's how not to give. Instead, he said, give like this: "But when you give to the needy, do not let your left hand know what your right hand is doing, so that your giving may be *in secret*. Then your Father, who sees what is done in secret, will reward you" (Matt. 6:3–4, emphasis mine). Jesus told them to raise the standard in their giving. Jesus was saying, "There is a standard of giving that is acceptable to some people, but you are held to a higher standard."

The entire sermon is like that. Jesus challenged them to raise the standard of their speech (taking oaths), of their prayer lives, of their commitments, of their choices (taking the narrow or wide road), of their influence (becoming salt and light), of their attitude toward God's Word, of their attitudes toward their enemies, of their priorities, of their ambitions (don't worry), and of their foundation (rock or sand), just to name a few.

In keeping with the raising the standard theme, Jesus discussed raising the standard of our character in the Beatitudes. Jesus began each of the Beatitudes with a word that is translated "blessed." The word used by Jesus to begin each Beatitude is *makarios* and is sometimes translated "happy".

The person who is blessed by God certainly has good reason to be happy, but to translate *makarios* as "happy' is to sell short the idea of being blessed by God. There is so much more to being blessed than being happy. Being blessed by God involves being approved by God. D. A. Carson wrote,

> Although some modern translations prefer "happy" to "blessed," it is a poor exchange. Those who are blessed will generally be profoundly happy; but blessedness cannot be reduced to happiness. . . . To be "blessed" means, fundamentally, to be approved, to find approval. . . .
>
> Since this is God's universe there can be no higher "blessing" than to be approved by God. We must ask ourselves whose blessing we diligently seek. If God's blessing means more to us than the approval of loved ones no matter how cherished, or of colleagues

no matter how influential, then the beatitudes will speak to us very personally and deeply.[1]

In other words, those who overcome fear of man seek God's approval. People who seek God's approval are wise to consider the actions and attitudes Jesus described as pleasing to God. God's sons and daughters who demonstrate these characteristics are blessed by the Father.

Recognized Spiritual Bankruptcy

"Blessed are the poor in spirit, for theirs is the kingdom of heaven" (Matt. 5:3). God approves of the person who recognizes his or her own state of sinfulness without the forgiveness of the Father. Jesus wasn't referring to the materially poor, but the spiritually poor. Without the grace of God demonstrated through his Son, you and I are spiritually bankrupt. Our cupboard is bare.

Now I realize there are some people who disagree. Some people believe we are good basically and have to be taught bad behavior, but people who believe that usually haven't had a lot of experience working with children.

Have you ever known anyone who had to teach their son or daughter to lie, especially if telling the truth might get the child into trouble? Did you have to teach your child to rebel against your authority with a defiant "No!"? Did you hold seminars for your little ones on being stingy and refusing to share with their siblings no matter how strong their inner urge to share and be generous was? (Why are you smiling?) Of course you didn't.

On the contrary, you have to encourage them to share, to tell the truth, and to yield to your authority. Ultimately that young person can be permanently changed only by God's Holy Spirit taking up residence in her life.

Here's something else you didn't do. When the child first began showing unacceptable behavior, like that described above, you didn't yell at him or her and say, "You lousy, degenerate, depraved human being." You didn't respond like that because you understood they came by those traits naturally, and so did you and I.

Your child is a work in progress. I like the child's T-shirt that reads: "Be patient with me. God's not through with me yet." In fact, a child who doesn't demonstrate inappropriate and unacceptable behavior periodically is the exception, not the rule.

So the proper place to begin in seeking the approval of the Lord is to recognize our utter dependence upon him with regard to our spiritual state. Overstating our desperation without him is impossible: "The heart is deceitful above all things and beyond cure. Who can understand it?" (Jer. 17:9).

Mourn Over Our Spiritual State Without God

"Blessed are those who mourn, for they will be comforted" (Matt. 5:4). Recognition of our sinfulness before our perfect heavenly Father is a good start but a far cry from repentance. Sometimes we mistake regret for being caught in a sin, for remorse over our sin. Perhaps we become sorry because we want to get rid of our feelings of guilt.

A man sent the Internal Revenue Service a one-hundred-dollar bill with an anonymous note that read: "This money is enclosed because I owe the government for back-taxes. I've lost sleep because of it. If after sending this amount I still can't sleep, I'll send the rest later." We would have to question the sincerity of the man's remorse.

Now I know reminding someone of his or her guilt isn't the popular thing to do. We're told to boost the self-esteem of others, not heap guilt on them. Frankly, I know of no greater boost to a person's self-esteem than to point them to the Cross.

Just think, here is a holy God who sends his One and Only Son to die a torturous death on a cross among thieves. The only explanation for that action is God's grace. He loved us and showed us his grace purely because that was his desire. Talk about a boost to one's self-image! God considered you and me worth the precious price he paid. We sing, "Jesus paid it all. All to him I owe. Sin had left a crimson stain. He washed it white as snow."

Still, even after we gain a sense of our spiritual poverty apart from God, and after we reach a condition of sorrow over our sinfulness in the face of God's grace, we haven't arrived at the place the Lord wants us. We must press on. In the Beatitudes, Jesus continued to take his listeners on a spiritual pilgrimage. Let's go to the next level.

Humble Yourself before God

"Blessed are the meek, for they will inherit the earth" (Matt. 5:5).

The next stage, after acknowledgment and sorrow over our sinful condition, is meekness. The word *meekness* may also be translated as "gentleness" or "humility." The Beatitudes represent an ascension of spiritual characteristics of which God approves. With regard to meekness, God shows his approval toward the humble by giving his grace. God opposes the proud but gives grace to the humble, and *grace* is another word for God's favor.

A mountain climbing guide was working his way up a mountain with his student-climber. Finally the two reached the top of the chilling peak. *Victory!* the student thought. The eager novice rushed past the experienced teacher and started to leap to his feet on the mountain's crest. Suddenly the teacher grabbed the student by the coat and pulled him to the ground and explained, "The winds swirl constantly up here. If you straighten up, you and I will be snatched off this peak. The only way to achieve greatness up here is to remain on your knees." "For whoever exalts himself will be humbled, and whoever humbles himself will be exalted" (Matt. 23:12).

If you think through what Jesus is said, the progression of his teaching in the Beatitudes makes sense. First, a person recognizes his or her spiritual bankruptcy apart from God. Second, this awareness leads to mourning because of his or her spiritual condition. Then, as a response to the only One who can rescue us from this state of depravity, the person humbles himself before God and receives grace.

I heard about a little boy who was shaking his pastor's hand as he left the church building after Sunday morning worship. The little boy said, "Pastor, that was a good sermon. You made my daddy sink *way* down in his seat today."

You're smiling—because we've all slumped now and then when we felt the familiar sting of conviction over our own sinfulness. Well, God's ultimate purpose in showing us our spiritual poverty is not only to make us feel guilty. He wants our condition to be changed, and we are changed when we humble ourselves before him.

Jesus told a story to some people who were confident of their own goodness and who looked down on others. There were three characters in the story: a Pharisee (a respected religious leader), a tax collector (the title itself was synonymous with being a sinner), and God (the one who could see inside the heart of both men).

The two men came into the temple to pray. The Pharisee stood boldly before the Lord and thanked God that he wasn't like other sinful people. The tax collector stood at a distance, beat his chest, and said, "God, have mercy on me, a sinner" (Luke 18:13).

The irony of the story is that God was not impressed with the good deeds of the Pharisee. The people in Jesus' audience were probably impressed. The Pharisees fasted twice a week. They gave money to the poor. Good deeds like that draw applause from people.

Jesus said the second man in the story, the one who humbled himself, left that place justified before God. Anyone looking on probably would not have applauded the brokenness of the man who acknowledged his sinful state, but God was pleased.

God said to the prophet Isaiah, "This is the one I esteem: he who is humble and contrite in spirit, and trembles at my word" (Isa. 66:2).

Crave Righteousness

"Blessed are those who hunger and thirst for righteousness, for they will be filled" (Matt. 5:6).

Only our heavenly Father can satisfy the deep spiritual yearning in our souls. On the morning of August 31, 1997, headlines around the world reported the tragic death of Diana, Princess of Wales. While vacationing in Paris with her companion, Dodi Fayed, the Princess, a bodyguard, and the driver of their car raced into a tunnel at an estimated speed of 120 miles per hour. They were reportedly trying to give camera-clicking paparazzi the slip.

The results of the pursuit were deadly. The car crashed into a concrete post in the center of the tunnel, killing Diana, Fayed, the driver, and seriously injuring the bodyguard. In the investigation, officials discovered the driver was driving under the influence of alcohol (his blood alcohol level was almost four times the French legal limit). What a waste—mostly for the pursuit of a profitable snapshot.

As tragic as the death of the young Princess was, our own pursuits can lead to results that are just as devastating. People who hunger for sensual satisfaction eventually find themselves diseased or emotionally broken. Those who pursue wealth leave a trail of casualties as a result of greed, misplaced priorities, and unnurtured relationships with those who love them. They seldom know the joy that can be experienced through showing generosity to someone else. People who long for education to satisfy an inner thirst must beware the snares of pride, loss of spiritual sensitivity, and cynicism. All of these pursuits are counterfeit. They are like salt water. They only create a thirst for more.

King Solomon learned the hard way that apart from God, everything is meaningless. It's not that there is anything wrong with experiencing some pleasure, or pursuing educational goals, or enjoying material possessions. Solomon also said there is a time to weep and a time to laugh, a time to mourn and a time to dance.

When our primary pursuit in life is to know God with all of our heart, then we can enjoy the other blessings of life. We can appreciate learning because we realize the fear of the Lord is the beginning of knowledge (Prov. 1:7). We can cherish experiences that bring us pleasure because we acknowledge God as the source of our joy in good and in difficult circumstances. We can appreciate having nice things because we realize every good and perfect gift comes from above, and we can give thanks to the one who provides all of life's blessings.

Jesus said, "But seek first his kingdom and his righteousness, and all these things will be given to you as well" (Matt. 6:33). Solomon and Jesus reached the same conclusion regarding what should be the primary aim of our pursuits: to fear God and keep his commandments (Eccles. 12:13b)—in other words, to hunger and thirst for righteousness.

Show Mercy

"Blessed are the merciful, for they will be shown mercy" (Matt. 5:7).

As I mentioned earlier, reading the Beatitudes is like ascending a staircase. There is a progression from the beginning to the end. To review, Jesus began by identifying the need for human beings to recognize spiritual bankruptcy without God's grace. Then he stressed the importance of possessing a holy grief over being separated from God. After mourning over our sin, we are to humble ourselves in meekness before God and begin a quest of thirsting after or pursuing righteousness that should be demonstrated in the life of God's children.

Next, Jesus described the three indicators that a person has had a change of heart and is hungering for the presence of God. The three indicators are showing mercy to others, being pure in heart, and making peace.

Remember, these are actions and attitudes that meet God's approval. Could the reason he approves of them be that he is so adept at these actions himself? Let's see if we can make out the reflection of his face as we look at the merciful, the pure in heart, and the peacemakers.

The word used in Matthew 5:7 for *mercy* can also be translated as "compassion." In other words, Jesus was saying that the person to whom God has shown mercy should show compassion toward others. Makes sense doesn't it? Out of a grateful heart, because we've been forgiven of so much, we in turn will forgive others. Could it be that some have a hard time being compassionate because they've tried to jump all the way to this step without spending time on the previous steps of the Beatitudes?

Jesus drove home a lesson about mercy with a stinging story in the home of a Pharisee. A hurting soul identified by Luke as "a sinful woman" heard Jesus was at the home. She went there and found Jesus.

Using her hair as an anointing cloth, she wiped a mixture of tears and fragrant perfume on Jesus' feet. When people have been shown compassion they look for ways to demonstrate love toward someone else. The perfume smelled sweet to Jesus but foul to the owner of the house.

Have you ever noticed that Jesus taught some of his greatest lessons by asking questions? "Do you want to get well?" "Which one of these three do you think was the man's neighbor?" "Whose image is on the coin?" This time was no exception.

Jesus told a story about two men who owed money to a certain moneylender. The first owed an enormous debt he could never repay. The second owed a meager amount. Neither of the men could pay the lender back so the lender canceled both debts. Jesus asked, "Now which of them will love him more?" There's the question (see Luke 7:36–47).

Simon, the head of the house answered correctly: "I suppose the one who had the bigger debt canceled." Jesus made his point. The woman's need for forgiveness was great. Actually, her need was no greater than the Pharisee's, but she acknowledged her need.

Jesus drove the lesson home saying, "Her many sins have been forgiven—for she loved much. But he who has been forgiven little loves little" (Luke 7:47). Then Jesus, the greatest forgiver of debts, turned to the woman and said, "Your sins are forgiven."

Sometimes people don't show mercy to others, even though they have been the recipients of compassion themselves. Jesus told another story about a man who did not show compassion.

A king wanted to settle accounts with his servants. He demanded that the first servant pay off a debt equivalent to millions of dollars. The man wasn't able to pay, so the king ordered the servant and his family be sold into slavery to repay the debt. The servant begged the king for more time. The king's heart softened. Out of compassion for the servant, the king forgave the debt. A nice story, right?

In the second phase of the story, Jesus set the hook. The servant whose debt had been wiped out found another servant who owed him the equivalent of a few dollars. The second servant made the same request as the first had made to the king—more time.

The first servant was unwilling to give more time to the second. Short memory, huh? He had the second servant thrown in jail. When the king heard of the first servant's actions, he had the man thrown in jail and tortured until he paid back all he owed. Jesus added, "This is how my heavenly Father will treat each of you unless you forgive your brother from your heart" (Matt. 18:35).

"Blessed are the merciful, for they will be shown mercy." Want the Father's approval? Show mercy to others the way he so faithfully shows mercy to us.

Possess Purity

"Blessed are the pure in heart, for they will see God" (Matt. 5:8).

One of the reasons we aren't as bold about our convictions as we would like to be is because we fear being ridiculed for our own faults and shortcomings. People who know us usually are aware of our imperfections, flaws, and inconsistencies.

We know the skeletons in our own closet. We think if we don't rock the boat for anyone else, maybe no one will dig too deeply into our life and reveal a character flaw, a weakness, or a failure in our past.

Think of the fear and guilt we carry around because our hearts are full of impurity. When King David tried to sweep his sins under the rug, he felt as if his bones were being crushed: "When I kept silent, my bones wasted away" (Ps. 32:3).

In contrast to the inner turmoil created by concealing sins, possessing a pure heart takes away fear and provides God's tender mercy. Listen to David express his desire for God's peace and comfort: "Let me hear joy and gladness; let the bones you have crushed rejoice" (Ps. 51:8).

I've never experienced more boldness in the pulpit (not belligerence, but confidence and assurance from the Lord) as when I knew I had been on my knees before our heavenly Father for a time of confession and cleansing. The prophet Ezekiel wrote, "Rid yourselves of all the offenses you have committed, and get a new heart and a new spirit" (Ezek. 18:31).

When your heart is full of God's grace and forgiveness, what is there to fear? When you honestly confess all faults and sin before God, you acknowledge to him that he knows the truth about you. His assessment of your sins is accurate, but he chooses to love you anyway. "He who conceals his sins does not prosper, but whoever confesses and renounces them finds mercy" (Prov. 28:13).

What does the opinion of others matter when you have admitted to the King of the Universe that without him you are nothing and have received his forgiveness and love? What confidence you can have—not in yourself, but in his grace. David sang, "Create in me a pure heart, O God, and renew a steadfast spirit within me" (Ps. 51:10).

One of my first decent jobs (at least I thought then the job paid good money) was an assistant manager's position for a grocery store chain. I hadn't worked for the company long when my eyes spotted a sporty new car I really liked. I had just moved to Mississippi, and the car I was driving at the time didn't even have air-conditioning.

You should have seen the new little coupe—power everything, sport mirror package, five-speed on the floor, sunroof. You name it, that car had all the bells and whistles. So I bought it. Actually I entered into a contract agreement with a bank to purchase the vehicle. OK, I was in debt up to my neck.

Then I learned the car had one thing I didn't want. One sunny afternoon I was driving home from work, and the car started sputtering and spitting and hesitating. I thought for a second I wasn't going to make it to the house.

Finally I took my sick patient to the car doctor. The diagnosis seemed serious to me: a clogged fuel filter. Then I saw the little gadget that was causing all the problems. Actually the filter was about the size of a human heart and was made out of plastic. The filter had water in it—enough to make the whole automobile virtually inoperable.

A man in an oily uniform with grease under his fingernails replaced the bad filter with a new one. The new part cost only a few dollars, and I was on my way. The car never ran better, and I was amazed at how such a small part could have such devastating effects on the operation of the vehicle.

Your heart does for your spirit what a fuel filter does for a car. It sifts out the impurities and helps the engine run smoothly. It helps the car do what its designers intended it to do. And if those impurities aren't dealt with, they affect the operation of the vehicle.

Jesus said, "For out of the overflow of the heart the mouth speaks" (Matt. 12:34b). Later he explained, "What goes into a man's mouth does not make him 'unclean,' but what comes out of his mouth, that is what makes him 'unclean'. . . . But the things that come out of the mouth come from the heart, and these make a man 'unclean'" (Matt. 15:11, 18).

If your heart is impure, you're not going to be the instrument the Master created you to be. You'll sputter spiritually, and if the problems aren't corrected you'll find yourself broken down on the side of the road.

Have you ever been there? Abandoned? Lonely? Desperate? In desperate times, isn't it a great feeling to look up and see a trusted friend coming to your aid—especially when you know this friend has a replacement part to the part that's gone bad? It's simple—God can give you a new heart. A pure heart.

Then, suppose that trusted friend (you remember, the one who came to help when you were broken down on the side of the road) not only fixed the broken-down vehicle, but also offered to get in the driver's seat and be your personal chauffeur. You might be glad at first, until you learn there is one catch— instead of taking you where you want to go, he takes you where he wants you to go.

Part of the responsibility of having a pure heart is trusting the one who gave it to you. A modern bumper sticker reads, "God is my copilot," but God doesn't just want to be our copilot. He wants to be the pilot, the copilot, the engineer, the navigator, the technician, and the air traffic controller. He wants absolute control over the direction and pattern of your life.

But here's great news: He'll never take you anywhere he is not present. He always sees what lies ahead. He designed your aircraft and knows best how to operate it. He's wiser than you are, and he has your best interest in mind as he guides your life. Go ahead and face it—your life is much safer in his hands than in your own. As kids we sang, "He's got the whole world in his hands." That truth is still comforting to me.

Before we move on, I want you to notice the reward promised to those who possess a pure heart: "They will see God." At one time this verse puzzled me. I have never known anyone who has seen God literally.

I've witnessed God's creation. I've seen his work in my own life. I've witnessed God through the behavior of others and through the miracles he's allowed me to witness. I've seen his work through the miracle of life as each of my four children came into the world. I've seen him change the hearts of people, giving husbands and wives new spouses, and giving boys and girls new mommies and daddies. But actually seeing God himself? Can't say that I have.

A pure heart allows you and me to see God, because we see him through eyes of faith. This hit me one day as I read through the "faith chapter," Hebrews 11. The author of Hebrews told how Moses refused to be known as the son of Pharaoh's daughter. He chose to be mistreated along with the people of God over the temporary pleasures provided by sin. He looked to the future for his reward, the author wrote.

The next part of chapter eleven is my favorite: "By faith he [Moses] left Egypt, not fearing the king's anger; he persevered because he saw *him who is invisible*" (Heb. 11:27, emphasis mine). Moses had seen God's hand in the form of signs. But the author of Hebrews commends Moses because of his faith. So, how do you see the one who is invisible? You see him through the eyes of faith.

Have you seen him? If you possess a pure heart you have. When your heart is made pure, you receive his love and grace. And although he is invisible, you know he is present. Then his presence affects every decision you make. You not only possess a pure heart in reality, but your life demonstrates that you have a new fuel filter. The engine runs like a top. You have a new pilot who's directing you on a new course. You trust him because he could not love you more than he does right now and because he never makes mistakes.

You don't have to wait for eternity to see the one who loves you enough to die for you. You can see him right now, by possessing a pure heart.

Make Peace

"Blessed are the peacemakers, for they will be called sons of God" (Matt. 5:9).

Richard Nixon's epitaph reads: "The greatest honor history can bestow is the title of peacemaker." But peacemakers usually don't draw attention to themselves. Troublemakers make the headlines: "Timothy Mcveigh and Terry Nichols charged in Oklahoma City bombing"; "Unabomber suspect arrested"; "Tyson bites Holyfield"; "Dennis Rodman head-butts official": OK, I think you've had enough.

Remember, in our study we're not concerned with getting the attention of human beings. In essence, Jesus said, "If you want to get God's attention, be a peacemaker." Paul wrote, "For God is not a God of disorder but of peace" (1 Cor. 14:33).

God pleasers can make peace in two ways. First, we can make peace between ourselves and others. Paul wrote, "If it is possible, as far as it depends on you, live at peace with everyone" (Rom. 12:18). This may not always be possible, but we are to put forth the effort.

Making peace doesn't come naturally for most of us. The concept of being a peacemaker is countercultural. We're expected to treat people the way they treat us. Somebody wants conflict between us and them? Fine by us. We'll gladly accommodate. He snubs me? I'll snub him back. That's what our culture expects. But the Lord tells us to live counterculturally.

Jesus said, "If you are offering your gift at the altar and there remember that your brother has something against you, leave your gift there in front of the altar. First go and be reconciled to your brother; then come and offer your gift" (Matt. 5:23–24). In other words, we're not to think about peace in the vertical relationship with God until we've made peace in our horizontal relationships with people.

The second way to be a peacemaker is to negotiate peace between other people or parties. This takes peacemaking to another level. Some of you have the tact and wisdom to reconcile disagreeing parties. May your tribe increase. You may not win many awards here on earth, but Jesus used a term to describe your lot—"sons of God." James wrote, "The seed whose fruit is righteousness is sown in peace by those who make peace" (James 3:18, NASB).

One final word on peacemaking. This seems almost too obvious to mention, but our heavenly Father is our perfect example of a peacemaker. The rift between humankind and God did not occur because he offended us. We offended him. He didn't cause the division between us and his creation. That was our doing. Our rebellion against him was red-handed mutiny.

Still, he pursued us anyway. He loved us. He desired to have peace with his children again, so he took the initiative. He didn't wait on us. He became proactive and mended our relationship. How? "By making peace through his blood, shed on the cross. Once you were alienated from God and were enemies in your minds because of your evil behavior. But now he has reconciled you by Christ's physical body through death to present you holy in his sight" (Col. 1:20–22).

The nails were not what held Jesus
to the cross on that glorious day.
It was his love for you and me that did it.
Oh, the love that drew salvation's plan.

Oh, the grace that bro't it down to man!
Oh, the might gulf that God did span
At Calvary.

—*W. R. Newell*

The Lord Is the Greatest Peacemaker of All

I can't fully explain everything that happened when Jesus gave his life on the cross. All I know is that I'm constantly seeing the effects of his selfless act in my own life. Let me illustrate by giving you an example of how Jesus has provided peace in my family.

If you have children, you have experienced the kind of Sunday morning that occurred recently while we visited my parents in Kentucky. You know the routine: "If I have to tell you one more time to go and brush your hair. . . .No, those socks do not match, go find the mate. . . .Because I said so. . . .Quit aggravating your little sister. . . . Eat your breakfast, we have to go. . . Try not to get any on your new dress. . . ."

How about this one: "You guys quit horsing around. We don't have time for that, and somebody is going to get hurt." That's the one I was trying to get out of my mouth, but it just wouldn't come fast enough. Before I could say it, I heard the crash in the bathroom and the thud of a skull against the side of the bathtub. What followed were screams that would have made Alfred Hitchcock proud.

Fortunately, no blood was lost, but we had a quiet ride to church. We attended the last of three morning worship services. The place was packed. While my wife took our daughter to the nursery and our three boys went to the rest room, old Dad's job was to save the seats. Have you ever tried to save four seats in a packed worship center just when the service is getting ready to start? It's survival of the fittest.

The troops returned from the rest room, but when they took their seats, our two oldest (the same two who had had the free-for-all in the bathtub) started to bicker about where each would sit, making a scene in front of all these well-dressed church folks and embarrassing their father. So I firmly took them by the arms and forced them to sit where I wanted them to sit (smiling all the while, of course, for those who could see but not hear what was going on).

This made them both angry, and they gave me a scowl that comes when children are angry at a parent but can't do anything about it. So, there we were in a great church, blowing an opportunity to worship as a family and hear a special word from the Lord.

The service started with a medley of moving praise choruses and hymns, but they had fallen flat. I prayed, "Lord, please don't let us blow this chance to worship you and hear a special word from you this morning. Forgive me for becoming angry and worrying about what others around me think. My sons are angry with me, and I'm outdone with them. Would you begin to soften our hearts so we won't be wasting our time here?"

Praying that prayer was the right thing to do, but I knew it would take a miracle to salvage the day. Then God provided the miracle. You won't be surprised to hear when the extraordinary event took place—during Communion.

With one son on my right side and the other on my left, we took the cracker and cup from the plate and held them. With music playing softly in the background, we took those precious elements and held them with our heads bowed and eyes closed. We took Communion too seriously to go any further while our hearts were in their present state.

I began to ponder the Cross again and the suffering Savior. My anger seemed all the more petty as I thought about his love for me. I know this sounds strange, but during that time of meditation and reflection, my heart was not the only one I felt soften. I knew theirs had, too. Both of my sons sat as close as they could to me, and I felt their tense muscles relax. I patted them both gently on their knees, and they rested their heads on my shoulders. The taste of the Communion bread and cup were never sweeter.

Here is what I wanted you to know about that experience. God provided his peace in the midst of our turmoil as we once again looked to the Cross. Our own self-centeredness was magnified as we considered the most selfless act ever performed. This dad was grateful again that the Lord is still the best peacemaker of all.

The Christmas chorus, "Gentle Mary Laid Her Child," describes in beautiful terms the peace God offers us through the giving of his son:

> *Gentle Mary laid her Child*
> *Lowly in a manger;*
> *There he lay, the undefiled,*
> *To the world a stranger:*
> *Such a Babe in such a place,*
> *Can he be the Savior?*
> *Ask the saved of all the race*
> *Who have found His favor.*
> *Gentle Mary laid her Child*
> *Lowly in a manger;*
> *He is still the undefiled,*
> *But no more a stranger:*
> *Son of God, of humble birth,*
> *Beautiful the story;*
> *Praise his name in all the earth,*
> *Hail the King of glory!*

> *—Joseph Simpson Cook*

Perhaps you have never known true peace in your life because you have never called on the name of the Prince of Peace—Jesus Christ. Would you like to confess to him your helplessness without him? Would you like to receive his gift of eternal life and permanent peace forever? By faith and repentance you can. "If you confess with your mouth, "Jesus is Lord," and believe in your heart that God raised him from the dead, you will be saved. For it is with your heart that you believe and are justified, and it is with your mouth that you confess and are saved" (Rom. 10:9–10).

Can you honestly say, "Yes, I'm at peace with God"? In June 1998, Maurice Hooks, a Jones County, Mississippi, sheriff, thought his life was over. While Hooks and a colleague were transporting prisoners from one facility to another, the inmates overpowered the two officers and took Hooks' pistol.

The inmates beat the sixty-year-old sheriff. Then they hand-cuffed the two men to two posts in an abandoned barn in the countryside. Hooks was certain he was done for. He pleaded with his captors to have mercy on his friend: "Leave this man alone. He's seventy years old, and he's sick." Then he made a final request, "If you're going to kill me, let me have a minute to make peace with God." Isn't it something how our priorities change when we think we only have a few moments to live?

After binding the mouths of the two men, the inmates jumped in the patrol car and sped away. As they were driving away, one of the inmates rolled down his window, pointed his finger at Hooks, and said, "Your faith just saved your life." Hooks and his friend were found the next day. They suffered minor injuries.

In the above story, Hooks' desire to make peace with God saved his life. I commend him for focusing on what's important during a time of crisis. But there is something far better than making peace with God when we face death: maintaining a relationship of peace with the Father all of the time.

Perhaps you cannot honestly say, "You know, if I were to die right now, I'm certain I am at peace with God. I know if I were to die today, I would go straight to be with God in heaven." If you aren't certain of your eternal destiny, you can be certain from this point on by making peace with the Prince of Peace.

According to God's Word, you and I can be certain of our eternal destiny. 1 John 5:13 reads, "I write these things to you who believe in the name of the Son of God so that you may *know* that you have eternal life" (emphasis mine). See? We don't have to speculate. We can know.

Would you like to be sure? Are you ready to confess your sins to the Father and ask him to give you eternal life with him in heaven? I'll help you if you would like. Here is a prayer much like the one I prayed years ago to respond to Jesus and experience his saving grace. You can do the same. Here's the prayer.

Let me be the first to welcome you to a new future. "If we confess our sins, he is faithful and just and will forgive us our sins and purify us from all unrighteousness" (1 John 1:9).

❧❧❧

Prayer

Dear God, I know I'm a sinner. I fall so short of your standard. Thank you for showing me I am spiritually bankrupt without you. Most of all, I confess my sin of unbelief that Jesus is the Christ, the Son of the living God. Please forgive me. Now I believe.

I believe that Jesus, your perfect Son, lived a perfect life and died a suffering death on a cross so that my sins would be forgiven. And I believe he was raised from the dead by your mighty power.

Please come into my life right now and change my heart. Cleanse me, Lord. If you clean me, I will be clean. Thank you for hearing my prayer and for forgiving my sin. I pledge from this day forward to live for you. In the name of your Son, my Lord and Savior, Jesus, I pray, Amen.

Summary

According to Jesus, you and I may take a course that pleases the Father. God approves of those who recognize and mourn over their own spiritual bankruptcy without him. He is pleased when we humble ourselves before him as the only one who can fill our empty bank account with the riches of his grace.

God's grace then creates a hunger and thirst for more of his blessing. He applauds those who crave to be more like his Son.

And since we have received his mercy, he shows favor to those who extend mercy to others.

In the next chapter we'll examine the results of and rewards for seeking heavenly approval over human applause. Since one of the potential results of seeking God's approval is persecution, we're going to wait until the next chapter to deal with the last beatitude: Blessed are those who are persecuted because of righteousness.

Chapter 6
Results of Pleasing the Father

*[Enoch] was commended as one who pleased God. And
without faith it is impossible to please God, because anyone
who comes to him must believe that he exists and that he
rewards those who earnestly seek him. (Heb. 11:5b–6)*

Seeking the approval of our heavenly Father occasionally
leads to immediate results, but often the rewards are delayed.
Some results are positive and some are negative. If we lived in
the best of all possible worlds, being faithful to God and seeking
his approval would have immediate and positive results always.
Most people desire swift rewards for obedience, but what if
judgment for disobedience came as swiftly as we wanted our
rewards from the Lord to come?

Sometimes God's discipline is swift. Ananias and Sapphira
attempted to deceive the Holy Spirit and were judged immediately. At other times, God is long-suffering. One hundred years
passed between the introduction of Noah in Genesis and the
time the first drop of rain fell. Most people scoffed at Noah's
warnings. God wasn't being aloof in holding off the rain. He
was practicing patience.

Personally, I'm grateful for God's patience. Aren't you glad
we don't always get what we deserve? I heard about an old lady
who asked a young artist who was painting her portrait,
"Young man do you think you can do me justice?" "Ma'am,"
the painter answered, "you don't need justice. You need

mercy." We may desire justice for others, but when it comes to God's treatment of us, most of us would rather have mercy.

God's distribution of rewards is similar to his disbursement of discipline—sometimes swift, but often unhurried. Let's look at some of the things that may take place when you do the right thing—when you seek the applause of God over the approval of others.

Condemnation by People

Acting to please our heavenly Father often leads to being on the receiving end of harsh treatment by others. My brother used to have a T-shirt that read, "Virtue is its own punishment." Unfortunately, as far as people are concerned, virtue is sometimes punished instead of rewarded.

Even when you and I are at peace with God, we may be at odds with other people. In fact, a result of your obedience to God may be persecution from others. So let's begin by examining the results of living a life that glorifies the Father.

According to Jesus, the Father approves of faithfulness in the face of persecution. He blesses those who suffer because of their faith in him. Your faithfulness may lead to the loss of a job or an opportunity. That hurts. But "Better a little with the fear of the LORD than great wealth with turmoil" (Prov. 15:16). No amount of material gain or prosperity is worth a break in your relationship with the Lord.

Please understand me here. Sometimes seeking God's approval over the approval of others is rewarded immediately and unmistakably. A friend and colleague of mine recently attended a professional meeting in Daytona Beach, Florida. Gene arrived at the hotel late, about 1:30 A.M., and went straight to the room to which he had been assigned.

The hotel was full, so he was assigned a roommate, who was attending the same function, for the week. There was one problem. When Gene got to his room, he discovered a slight error had been made.

Since his name was Gene, the hotel management assumed he was a female and assigned him a female roommate. The surprised woman was already in her nightgown when an unsuspecting, wide-eyed college professor entered the room.

Trying to make the best out of an embarrassing situation, the woman suggested Gene stay in the room anyway. There was another bed, after all, and it was late, etc. My married friend declined and left the room immediately. In addition to being married, he was a Christian who wanted to avoid any appearance of evil.

The woman probably thought he was a prude. The hotel management faced a logistical nightmare since there were no other rooms available. None. What could they do? Gene didn't compromise. He just waited. Then a solution came. The hotel clerk located a room in another hotel for my friend, but this one did not come with its own roommate.

Gene spent the week in a *presidential suite*! The room included a balcony with a view overlooking the beach. It was a tough assignment, but somebody had to do it. In Gene's case, his commitment to his family and the Lord and his disregard for what people thought about his decision were rewarded immediately. Rewards for faithfulness do not always come as swiftly.

A young man by the name of Joseph in the Old Testament made a decision similar to Gene's with devastating results. Joseph was sold into slavery by his older brothers. His owners took Joseph to Egypt, far from his home and his father, and sold him to Potiphar, the captain of Pharaoh's bodyguards.

Potiphar respected Joseph, and the kid earned his master's trust. Potiphar put Joseph in charge of his whole household. The writer of Genesis wrote, "With Joseph in charge, [Potiphar] did not concern himself with anything except the food he ate" (Gen. 39:6). The only thing in the entire house that was off-limits to Joseph was the wife of his master.

The plot thickens. Joseph was well-built and handsome, and eventually Potiphar's wife tried to seduce him. Even in the face of temptation, this young man was faithful to Potiphar. More importantly he was faithful to God. Joseph faced a dilemma: *Do I yield to this woman's invitation and win her approval, or do I yield to God's will for me to remain pure and faithful and gain God's approval?*

Like my friend Gene, Joseph chose God's favor, but unlike my friend, Joseph suffered severe consequences for his decision. In her last attempt to seduce Joseph, Potiphar's wife grabbed him by his cloak and said, "Lie with me." The young man literally shed his cloak and ran away.

After being rejected, the woman used Joseph's cloak to ruin his reputation. She made up a story and told her husband that Joseph had tried to seduce her. She told her husband she screamed for help and Joseph ran away, leaving his garment behind.

What was Joseph's reward for seeking God's approval? Prison for two years—two years of his prime. While other Hebrew young men his age were building their own families and climbing the ladder of success, Joseph waited in obscurity in a dungeon.

But Joseph wasn't the only one who was trustworthy and faithful—so was his heavenly Father. God wasn't sitting on his hands. He wasn't asleep. He wasn't on vacation. He simply had a different timetable than Joseph. He had higher plans for this innocent young man. Isn't that encouraging? The Lord told Isaiah, "My ways [are] higher than your ways and my thoughts than your thoughts" (Isa. 55:9).

Joseph could have related to the apostle Paul's words, "And we know that God causes all things to work together for good to those who love God, to those who are called according to His purpose" (Rom. 8:28, NASB). Paul and Joseph were no strangers to persecution. They suffered pain and ridicule because they sought to please God rather than people.

Even in prison, Joseph experienced the hand of God working in his life. He interpreted a couple of dreams for his cell mates.

One of his fellow prisoners was executed, but the other was released. The released prisoner was the cupbearer of the king, but after being released from the dungeon, he didn't give any thought to Joseph until two years later.

Like the cupbearer, Pharaoh had a couple of dreams, too. When the king's magicians and soothsayers were unable to interpret Pharaoh's dreams, the cupbearer remembered Joseph. He told Pharaoh about the gifted inmate, and Pharaoh sent for Joseph. After hearing the dreams explained, Joseph interpreted them for the king.

Joseph's explanation of the dreams was that a famine was going to occur after seven years of prosperity. Pharaoh needed to begin preparing immediately so they would survive the crisis to come.

Pharaoh appointed Joseph as administrator of the project to save not only the people of Egypt, but also other nations in the region who felt the effects of the same drought. Through Joseph's efforts Egypt was not only saved—she prospered. Joseph became second in command, accountable only to Pharaoh himself. And even better, Joseph was eventually reconciled with his estranged family.

I'd say Joseph's faithfulness paid off—but not right away. His reward didn't come as quickly as my friend Gene's, but the results for the young man and his fellow Hebrews were far greater than a week in a presidential penthouse. God has his own special plan for your life—a plan so unique, only he could design it, and his timing is always better than ours.

As far as suffering for doing good is concerned, please remember a couple of things. First, Jesus suffered far more than you or I probably ever will. No servant is greater than his or her master. Jesus learned obedience from his suffering (Heb. 5:8), and so will we.

Second, God matures us in part through suffering. Suffering has the potential to mature our character that nothing else does. "Not only so, but we also rejoice in our sufferings, because we know that suffering produces perseverance; perseverance, character; and character, hope" (Rom. 5:3–4). C. S. Lewis called suffering "God's megaphone." He calls to us in our suffering.

A third thing to remember regarding suffering is this: God *always* rewards those who are faithful—period. If He doesn't reward you now, he will later. "Now if we are children, then we are heirs—heirs of God and co-heirs with Christ, if indeed we share in his sufferings in order that we may also share in his glory. I consider that our present sufferings are not worth comparing with the glory that will be revealed in us" (Rom. 8:17–18).

Our attitude about serving God and not people is so critical. If our service is only for people, we have to depend on people for our reward. Often a reward will not come at all. Even when people *do* reward and applaud you, the favor of people is nothing compared to God's blessing. Human approval is temporary; God's approval is eternal. "Serve wholeheartedly, as if you were serving the Lord, *not men*, because you know that the Lord will reward *everyone* for whatever good he does" (Eph. 6:7–8, emphasis mine).

The Blessings of God's Favor

The blessings experienced by the Christian who does not yield to the fear of man are similar to the blessings experienced by Jesus. In a previous chapter, I mentioned that Jesus saw three major results because he sought to please the Father: hearing the affirming voice of the Father, seeing signs and wonders, and experiencing his miraculous resurrection.

First, Jesus was affirmed by the words of his Father: "This is my Son, whom I love; with him I am well pleased" (Matt. 3:17).

Some believers may receive audible affirmation from the Lord himself, but all of us have the affirmation of his written Word. One Christian author described the promises of God as ripe fruit falling from the pen of the biblical authors. Sometimes through Scripture or through the inner voice of the Holy Spirit within us, God's voice is louder than any audible voice.

Another result of Jesus' seeking his Father's approval was the manifestation of miracles. Do miracles still happen? You bet they do? Are they commonplace? No. That's why they are called miracles and not "normals."

Recently my dear friend, Bruce Brady, called me and told me a story I will never forget about God's wonderful healing power. I could never improve on Bruce's version of the story. I asked him to write down what happened to his father (who also is named Bruce, but is affectionately called "Pap" by family members and friends). I share the story with you with Bruce's permission:

> My father was diagnosed with terminal cancer back in September, 1997. There is no cure for this type of cancer and the average life expectancy is about 12 to 18 months. The doctors hoped to slow down the growth of the cancer through chemo and radiation. Less than 50 percent of the people treated see positive results. None are cured totally by the treatment.
>
> From day one we prayed for God's healing, but the Lord began to deal with me about the way I had been praying for my dad. In all honesty, I had been trying to "save face" for God as I prayed. I didn't want God to look bad if my father wasn't healed. I prayed with "strings attached," so to speak.
>
> The Lord revealed to me that he did not need me to save face for him! He is God regardless of what anyone else thinks. I was reminded that I am to come boldly before his throne.
>
> I remembered how when David faced Goliath, he didn't say, "*If* it is the Lord's will, I will defeat you today." David said, "I come before you in the name of the Lord of hosts, the God of the armies of Israel. This day the Lord will deliver you into my hands, and I will strike you down. . . ."
>
> On March 17, 1998, I went by my parents' home on the way to the office (as I do nearly every morning) to drink a cup of coffee and pray for my father's healing. I shared my thoughts concerning the way I had been praying with my dad. He agreed—God was God, no matter what.
>
> As we stood in his driveway that morning, I turned to him and said, "Pap, today is a day of rejoicing, because the Lord has healed you!" (The words shocked me. I thought, "Did I just say that?")

Pap's response was, "If it's the Lord's will, that's right." And I said, "No, Pap, you don't get it. The Lord has healed you this day!" He was speechless. We stood in the driveway and cried and embraced.

A few hours later, my dad went for his CAT. scan to determine where we stood in his fight with cancer. The technician laid him on the examination table and told him to hold his arms over his head.

As he was slid into the scanning machine, he closed his eyes and began to think about Jesus' suffering. He thought, "My suffering is so insignificant compared to the pain the Lord endured for me on the cross."

Then the Holy Spirit reminded Pap of Isaiah 53:5, By His stripes we are healed. My father says, at that moment, he felt a cold chill from his fingertips to his toes! He whispered, "Lord, did you just heal me?"

Then a second chill swept across his face. He said it was like the Lord saying, "Yes, you are healed." The technician finished the scan and everyone waited for the doctor's report.

When the doctor came into the room with the family, she said, "We have scheduled three more rounds of chemo for you, but you may want to go home and think about whether to take the treatments. Because there is no sign of cancer anywhere in your body." The doctors confirmed what we had already claimed and believed by faith.

I don't know why God chooses to perform miracles on some occasions and on others he doesn't. In his wisdom, that's how he deals differently with us and our circumstances. But I know miracles still happen.

In fact, we probably witness more miracles than we realize. We sometimes miss the miracles because people are so quick to explain away the unexplainable: We must have misdiagnosed the disease." "Well, you know, she changed after she got religion." "We weren't expecting that check in the mail, but it couldn't have come at a better time. What a coincidence."

Miracles still happen, probably more often than we realize. But Jesus commended those who believed despite the absence of physical "evidence." Thomas, the disciple who doubted, wasn't present the first time Jesus appeared to his disciples after the resurrection.

When he finally saw Jesus, Thomas said, "My Lord and my God!" Jesus said to Thomas, "Because you have seen me, you have believed; *blessed* are those who have not seen and yet have believed" (John 20:29, emphasis mine). Did you notice the term *blessed?* We could read the verse, *"Approved by God* are those who have not seen and yet have believed.*"*

I doubt that seeing supernatural signs and wonders would cause many people to believe Jesus was God in the flesh. Jesus told of the rich man and Lazarus. The rich man, who was in torment, pleaded for Lazarus to go back to the earth. The rich man had five brothers, and he didn't want them to be sent to this place of suffering.

The rich man thought his brothers might believe if someone were to rise from the dead. "'No, father Abraham', he said, 'but if someone from the dead goes to them, they will repent.' He said to him, 'If they do not listen to Moses and the Prophets, they will not be convinced even if someone rises from the dead'" (Luke 16:30–31).

Jesus was right. Someone *did* rise from the dead—Jesus himself—and still, some did not believe. Some still don't. That leads us to the third result I mentioned previously of Jesus' seeking God's favor—his resurrection from the dead.

The miracle of Jesus' resurrection is the greatest miracle of all. And all those who receive God's gift of salvation through his Son will experience a glorious resurrection too. "But Christ has indeed been raised from the dead, the *firstfruits* of those who have fallen asleep" (1 Cor. 15:20, emphasis mine).

The word for firstfruits in 1 Corinthians 15, was a term used for anything set apart for God before the remainder could be used. The word also implied a pledge or guarantee of what was to come later.

In other words, before you and I can inherit the eternal, we have to be delivered from the temporal. Before we can possess that which is perfect, we must shed that which is flawed, namely these bodies of flesh and blood. "Flesh and blood cannot inherit the kingdom of God, nor does the perishable inherit the imperishable. . . .In a flash, in the twinkling of an eye, at the last trumpet. For the trumpet will sound, the dead will be raised imperishable, and we will be changed. For the perishable must clothe itself with the imperishable, and the mortal with immortality" (1 Cor. 15:50, 52–53).

Jesus' resurrection was a prototype (the first thing or being of its kind) of our resurrection. He defeated death, and if we put our faith in him, we will, too—not because of our own effort, but because he was the firstfruits, a pledge of what was to come. "But thanks be to God! He gives us the victory through our Lord Jesus Christ" (1 Cor. 15:57).

I've mentioned the three *major* results of Jesus' seeking the Father's favor, both in the life of Christ and in the lives of those who follow after him. But these are broad categories: God's affirming words, miraculous deeds, and glorious resurrection. The ways God brings about these blessings are demonstrated in various ways in the lives of those who long for God's favor.

So let's see some particular results that can be experienced by those who seek God's applause rather than the applause of the world. These are only a few examples, but hopefully they will serve to make you keenly aware of how God is working in your own life as you desire his blessing and seek his will.

Exoneration by God

"Therefore, there is now no condemnation for those who are in Christ Jesus" (Rom. 8:1).

Seeking the approval of God sometimes leads to criticism, ridicule, and even persecution from other people, but God always has the last say. Sometimes He chooses to exonerate on earth the one who seeks his approval. But often his servant is not vindicated until eternity.

Bob Russell, pastor of the Southeast Christian Church in Louisville, Kentucky, told the story of a woman he called "Mary." She was pursuing a doctorate in psychology at a university in the Midwest. She was required to do a clinical skills portfolio in human nature psychopathology and psychotherapy—in other words, who we are, why we get sick, and how we get well. Most importantly, Mary is a dedicated believer in the Lord Jesus Christ.

When Mary handed in her first presentation to the university supervision group, she encountered opposition. The controversy was over her theory of human nature. She believed that humans were basically sinful and needed to be redeemed by God. Her supervisor told her there was no place for that kind of paper in their psychology program. She should have gone to seminary if she wanted to write something like that. Privately, the supervisor told Mary, "You're going to have to get *that* part out of the paper, or you will not pass."

While other students were encouraged in their regular two-hour sessions, Mary was belittled and warned again that her paper was unacceptable. The ridicule was so great that two students who were Christians in the group deleted any reference to Christianity in their papers. They feared being mocked. And they weren't confident they could defend their statements.

Mary began to pray about how she would handle her dilemma. She didn't want to be an obnoxious woman. In fact, normally she was gentle and unassuming. She concluded Christ would not have her back down from what she knew to be true. She determined she was out to please God and not people. The chips would have to fall where they would.

Two weeks before her final oral exam, one of her fellow students who was an unbeliever said, "You'd better take that stuff out, or they are going to rip you to shreds." But when the final came, Mary said, "God *did* go before me, and I did successfully defend the paper." Only three questions were asked, and she passed unconditionally.

That's not the end of the story, though. Later that university developed a colloquium, which Mary was asked to help lead. The seminar was intended to talk to students about how to have spiritual components in their clinical skills. The seminar was designed to help students realize that religion is another expression of human diversity, and it deserves to be heard and valued.

It gets better. Mary's paper was so well written, it is now being used by other students as an example of how to write a proper paper. Remember the student who ridiculed her and said, "You're going to be ripped to shreds"? Well, he didn't pass. In fact, the professors examining him assigned Mary's paper to him as an example of how to write a paper appropriately.[1]

Mary was vindicated quickly for her obedience. You may not be. Compared to the suffering experienced by many who have sought God's approval, Mary's was mild. Think of the people in Scripture who said no to human applause and looked to heaven for approval, but who never received their reward while on earth.

Abraham believed God and followed him. He was faithful to God in offering his son Isaac as a sacrifice, but he roamed the earth without a permanent home. This man who would be known as the father of a multitude was promised all of Israel, but when he died the only land he owned was the little plot where he had buried his wife, Sarah.

Stephen, the first Christian martyr, decided to speak the truth about the love God showed the world through his Son, instead of remaining silent to gain the approval of the religious authorities. In fact, those early believers considered suffering for the name of Christ a privilege (cf. Acts 5:41). The enemies of the gospel hurled stones at Stephen until he was dead.

A casual observer of these stories might think, "If that is the result of pleasing God, no thanks!" But the success of Abraham, Moses, Stephen, and scores of others is not measured by the standards used by many to measure significance. There is actually only one criterion for success: obedience to our heavenly Father. Just like Jesus, we learn obedience in part through our suffering.

The glorious truth about the rewards received by these giants of the faith is that they did reach their goal. They did cross the finish line. Their finish line was just a little farther up the road than it appeared, that's all.

That great theologian, Yogi Berra, is credited with saying, "It ain't over 'til it's over." Measuring the lives of God's children by what happens on earth is like watching a football or basketball game and determining that whichever team is ahead at the end of the third quarter is the winner. Nobody does that. Anything can happen in the final period.

I'm originally from Kentucky and grew up a devoted fan of the University of Kentucky Wildcat basketball program. A couple years ago, my wife and I were invited by some dear friends to go with them to Baton Rouge and watch the Wildcats play the Louisiana State University Tigers. Our friends were (and still are) huge LSU fans and supporters.

We settled into our seats to endure the second half. I still am not quite sure what happened. It was as if the teams had changed uniforms during the half-time break. Kentucky started cutting into the lead—25 points down, 20 points, 10 points, 2 points.

Finally, U of K won the game on a last second three–point shot by Walter McCarty. We later learned that the thirty-one-point comeback was the greatest second-half comeback in college basketball history.

Everybody loves a comeback, but I learned a couple of valuable lessons that night. First, *never give up*. Anything can happen. But I think the second lesson was more important: *Those who persevere to the end will receive a reward.*

If the ball game had ended at half-time, the results would have been completely different; but it didn't. If our lives ended when we die, some of our stories would be tragic indeed. Our lives here on earth are only a small part of a much larger picture. As a matter of fact, compared to eternity, the seventy, eighty, or even one hundred years we spend here on earth are only a drop in the bucket.

I mentioned a moment ago people like Moses, Abraham, and Stephen who fixed their eyes on a finish line farther ahead than many runners stretch for. Their heavenly reward was greater than any earthly prize. No human honor could equal their heavenly glory. In the song "I Am Not Ashamed of the Gospel," The Brooklyn Tabernacle Choir sings, "I'm not out to please the whole world around me. I've got my mind on eternity."

Abraham never saw his descendants, whom God said would be as great in number as the stars in the sky, but God gave him a greater reward. Now Abraham is the father not only of the Jewish people, but of all believers (see Rom. 4:16–17).

Moses saw the promised land, the land flowing with milk and honey, from a distance, but it was only a shadow of the real promise land. Now he receives his mail at a heavenly address. He left the treasures of Egypt for only a short time. From now on he will walk on streets of gold for eternity. Some trade, huh?

Stephen never occupied a seat of honor on the Sanhedrin, the religious Supreme Court of Israel. Nobody ever stood to honor him when he entered a room. But just before his death, Stephen looked into heaven and saw Jesus standing at the right hand of God. It must have been as if Jesus was saying, "I approve of your faithfulness, son. Come home and live with me." Stephen experienced something better than a seat of honor on earth. He took his seat at the banquet table of Christ.

The land where these heroes of the faith now live has no borders. The sun never rises nor sets, because the Son provides enough light for all of heaven. Was their suffering worth it? You bet it was. And yours will be too. You watch. You wait. You'll see.

"Blessed is a man who perseveres under trial; for once he has been *approved*, he will receive the crown of life, which the Lord has promised to those who love Him" (James 1:12, NASB; emphasis mine).

Heed Paul's encouraging words: "Let us not become weary in doing good, for at the proper time we will reap a harvest if we do not give up" (Gal. 6:9).

Summary

"But if when you do right and suffer for it you take it patiently, you have God's approval" (1 Pet. 2:20b RSV).

When you seek God's approval, you may experience ridicule and criticism from people, but God will exonerate you. Your obedience will not go unnoticed nor unrewarded. If your reward comes here on earth, be grateful. Give God the glory for it. If the reward doesn't come until eternity, please know this: When God rewards his children, he does it right. He is the best gift-giver there is.

Set your eyes ultimately on eternal things above, not the perishable rewards of the here and now. Don't long for treasures that will not last. Follow the example of the saints of old who discovered this earth would pass away. "They were longing for a better country—a heavenly one. Therefore God is not ashamed to be called their God, for he has prepared a city for them" (Heb. 11:16).

Evangelism

When God's people overcome their concern about what others think of them, they joyfully share God's good news of forgiveness and grace through His Son. When the good news is shared, many who hear will be saved.

Most people aren't going to accidentally stumble over the good news of salvation through Jesus Christ. Some people may wander in the basic direction of heaven, but most need someone else to show them the right way. They need someone to tell them.

While my family and I were serving our second church, a wonderful little church in the country, we had a standing invitation to eat Sunday lunch with Mrs. Elise Sartin and her family. Elise was a widow who cooked Sunday lunch every week for her large family and anyone else who wanted to come by.

Elise would serve roast, ham, rice and gravy, sweet potatoes, fresh black-eyed peas, butter beans, corn from her garden, homemade rolls, and those cornbread sticks that look like little ears of corn. Have I made you hungry yet?

Our first week in the community, Elise said, "Preacher, I'm inviting you and your family to eat with my family every single week after church. Don't wait on an invitation every week—this is it. If I change my mind, I'll tell you." Her invitation was so assertive, I found myself calling her and asking permission to miss a day when we were going to be out of town or when we had made other plans for lunch.

One Sunday on our way to Elise's house, Page and I noticed our four-year-old and six-year-old boys being unusually quiet. We enjoyed the little game they played each week, hiding behind the back seat of our mini van to make us think we were leaving them. We would say (loud enough for them to hear of course), "Well, I guess the boys just won't have lunch today. I guess they'll have to do without."

Usually the boys would let out a snicker of laughter and give themselves away, but after we had traveled a short distance on this particular day they were still silent.

Page and I made eye contact about the same time, as if to say to one another, "No. We couldn't have." But we had. It was like a scene straight from a Home Alone movie. We turned the van around and headed home. When we were approaching our house, we spotted both of the little fellows, walking hand in hand across a field in the general direction of Mrs. Sartin's place.

The two boys had made the trip enough that they knew basically which direction to begin walking, but Elise's house was miles away through the winding roads. They would have never made it without someone showing them the way. When we finally picked up the boys, they were a little ticked off as I recall, but they were glad they weren't on their own anymore.

You probably know people right now who need you to show them the way. They need you to point them to Jesus. Oh, they may be able to wander in the general direction of being a "good person," but faith comes by hearing. And they need to hear from you. "How can they believe in the one of whom they have not heard? . . . How beautiful are the feet of those who bring good news!" (Rom. 10:14–15).

When you tell others the good news, they may not approve of you at first. Initially, they may act offended, but allow the Holy Spirit room to work in the life of that person. God will provide a harvest in his time. Our role is to plant the seed.

By the way, please remember that when you do overcome your initial uneasiness, share the gospel with a measure of grace and truth. Your determination to obey God rather than please people will result in a freedom to share the gospel with others in a way you've probably never experienced before.

When you experience this freedom, however, please remain sensitive to those who are still bound by what's culturally "acceptable." Try to put yourself in their shoes. It isn't every day they meet someone who unashamedly shares their faith. They may be shocked at first.

I question the authenticity of this story, but I've heard that some engineers at NASA were testing the windshield of the space shuttle to ensure that the windshield could stand up to the impact of birds while in flight. The engineers designed a type of cannon that shot chickens at the front of the shuttle to simulate birds hitting the windshield at about the same velocity.

The device worked so well for NASA that Boeing officials who were designing a new jet wrote to the people at NASA and asked for the designs of the chicken gun. After assembling the gun, the Boeing officials conducted their own tests, but with disastrous results.

The propelled chicken had so much momentum behind it that it went through the windshield of the plane, then passed through the instrument panel, the pilot's seat, and finally roosted in the passenger compartment.

The Boeing officials immediately wrote NASA, describing the results of their tests and asking for advice on what to do next. The response of the NASA officials was brief. They wrote: "Dear Friends, Thaw out Chicken."

Even when our motives are good, if we go barreling forward and do not season the proclamation of truth with a measure of grace, we may do more damage than good. Jesus consistently exercised the perfect balance. That's why he came. "The Word became flesh and made his dwelling among us. We have seen his glory, the glory of the One and Only, who came from the Father, full of grace and truth. . . . For the law was given through Moses; grace and truth came through Jesus Christ" (John 1:14, 17).

Jesus balanced truth and grace with people, but he didn't compromise his convictions. Jesus offered a new birth to Nicodemus without approving of his pride. He offered a Samaritan woman living water, but not before confronting her with her lifestyle of going from one empty relationship to another. He went into the home of Zaccheus, but did not approve of the tax collector's dishonesty. Jesus tenderly forgave a woman caught in adultery, but told her to leave behind her sinful lifestyle. Do you see the perfect balance? Truth and grace.

But remember, our responsibility is to share: God takes it from there. And not everyone will respond in a positive manner. When Jesus offered the rich young ruler salvation, the young man turned the Lord down. Jesus told his disciples, "He who listens to you listens to me; he who rejects you rejects me; but he who rejects me rejects him who sent me" (Luke 10:16).

Regardless of how people respond to your sharing the good news about Jesus with them, your heavenly Father will approve. Remember, we are seeking **his** approval more than the approval of others.

Godly Wisdom

"The fear of the LORD is the beginning of wisdom; all who follow his precepts have good understanding. To him belongs eternal praise" (Ps. 111:10).

"Do not be wise in your own eyes; fear the LORD and shun evil" (Prov. 3:7).

In contrast to living for human approval, or the "fear of man", biblical writers commend people who have a healthy "fear" or reverence for God and seek his approval. According to the psalmist, the person who shows reverence for the Lord by keeping his precepts has discovered the beginning of wisdom.

Wisdom and knowledge are not the same. Wisdom is distinct from knowledge. The two terms are not synonymous. There is no lack of information and knowledge in the land, but godly wisdom is not as plentiful.

You and I live in a remarkable age. We have, literally at our fingertips, access to libraries of information. Through modern technology and the internet, one can do research in a day's time that used to take a team of researchers months to accomplish. But despite all the miles we've logged on the information highway, our appetite for understanding has not been satisfied.

Our age is the most educated in history, but it is more violent, and in many ways more evil, than any previous generation. Now, I am in the field of education. I've been in school most of my life. But if we don't realize God is the source of all truth, all of our learning is futile.

History is full of examples of intelligent, educated people, some who have made significant contributions, some who self-destructed. I want to take just a moment to remind you of two men who serve as examples of the futility of education apart from God. This isn't pleasant for me. The very mention of their names will make some of you cringe, because you remember the pain these men caused in the lives of others.

Ted Bundy and Ted Kaczynski had at least two things in common. They were both convicted of being mass murderers, and they were both highly educated. Bundy had a law degree. Friends called him brilliant. Kaczynski was a Harvard graduate.

Bundy's law degree and charismatic personality helped him gain the confidence of his victims. By the time they learned the truth about his evil nature, it was too late. Bundy eventually was killed by lethal injection in a Florida prison.

Kaczynski's knowledge of explosives and physics made him a danger to others. In his paranoia, he considered technology and experts in the field of technology a threat to society, so he began sending bombs by mail. Some of his victims lost their limbs or facial features. Others lost their lives.

Please understand where I'm coming from. Education and knowledge can be wonderful tools to do good in our world. But apart from God, education can lead to sorrow. Solomon discovered the futility of knowledge and conventional "wisdom" apart from God. In his personal journal he wrote, "For with much wisdom comes much sorrow; the more knowledge, the more grief" (Eccles. 1:18).

When I served a church in south Mississippi, I had a deacon named Mr. Rich Ladner. Rich was a real character and a retired school teacher. He was so encouraging to me when I was doing my work at the seminary. When time for final exams came around every semester, Rich could sense my anxiety level go up dramatically. He would remind me to keep things in perspective with the following saying: "Now Les, you need to remember, the more you study, the more you know. The more you know, the more you can forget. The more you forget, the less you know. So why study?" Then he would turn the little proverb around and say, "And the less you study, the less you know. The less you know, the less you can forget. The less you forget, the more you know. So why study?"

Since Rich was an educator himself, I knew his proverb was said tongue-in-cheek, but his sense of humor helped me keep things in perspective. With regard to knowledge, I wouldn't go to the extreme of Rich's proverb. That would be throwing the baby out with the bath water. Education has opened up some wonderful doors of opportunity for me, but education by itself is meaningless. In order for our lives to have meaning, we need God's wisdom.

> Where is the wise man? Where is the scholar? Where is the philosopher of this age? Has not God made foolish the wisdom of the world? For since in the wisdom of God the world through its wisdom did not know him, God was pleased through the foolishness of what was preached to save those who believe. . . . For the foolishness of God is wiser than man's wisdom, and the weakness of God is stronger than man's strength.

> Brothers, think of what you were when you were called. Not many of you were wise by human standards; not many were influential; not many were of noble birth. But God chose the foolish things of the world to shame the wise; God chose the weak things of the world to shame the strong. (1 Cor. 1:20–21, 25–27)

> My message and my preaching were not with wise and persuasive words, but with a demonstration of the Spirit's power, so that your faith might not rest on men's wisdom, but on God's power. (1 Cor. 2:4–5)

In our age of bits and bytes, hard drives and software, CDs and diskettes, our focus shouldn't be on having the right internet server, but on having an internal desire to serve the one who gives eternal wisdom. If any of you lacks wisdom, he should ask God, who gives generously to all without finding fault, and it will be given to him. . . . But the wisdom that comes from heaven is first of all pure; then peace-loving, considerate, submissive, full of mercy and good fruit, impartial and sincere. (James 1:5; 3:17)

> My son, if you accept my words and store up my commands within you, turning your ear to wisdom and applying your heart

to understanding, and if you call out for insight and cry aloud for understanding, and if you look for it as for silver and search for it as for hidden treasure, then you will understand the fear of the LORD and find the knowledge of God. (Prov. 2:1–5)

Earthly degrees are satisfying if the approval of people is all we desire. But if our desire is to hear the applause of our heavenly Father, knowledge alone won't cut it. Like Solomon said, more knowledge, apart from God, only leads to more grief. But those who seek God's approval are given wisdom, which leads to showing mercy and bearing good fruit for him.

Contentment with Possessions

One surprising benefit of seeking God's approval over the applause of human beings is a content state of mind, especially regarding possessions and circumstances. Modern advertisers use the need that you and I have for the approval of others as a tool to sell their products.

These experts in human nature tell us their product will make us more attractive, or more successful looking, or more confident. They capitalize on our discontentment.

Has this ever happened to you? I can be perfectly content with the clothes in my closet, or the furniture in my den, or the computer in my study. Then I begin thumbing through a catalog and I begin noticing all the things I "need". I tell myself, "It sure has been a long time since I've had a new suit. I'd look pretty good in that." "We need new furniture. That would give the den a much better look." "My computer met my needs when I bought it, but now it's way too slow, the resolution isn't clear enough, and it doesn't have enough memory."

What happened?! One minute I was satisfied and content, and the next I was thinking about maxing out my Visa. I'll tell you part of what contributed to my discontentment. One moment I was looking at what I had and the next I was noticing what I didn't have.

The truth is I have way more stuff than I actually need. When I become discontent, in reality I'm saying, "God, you have not met all my needs. In my opinion I need more. I want more."

A couple of years ago, I began looking for a pickup truck. I told myself, "Well, you know, as much as I hunt—and now the boys are old enough to go with me . . . It's time I got something to put the ATV and other equipment in so we don't tear up the car. We don't need anything fancy—just something to get us there." Right.

You should have heard the rationalizing going on in my head. It went something like this: "Boy, you just can't find a good *used* truck these days. They are either too expensive or they have too many miles on them. And you know this third door for the backseat sure is a neat feature. With four kids, I need that third door, which only the *new* models have, by the way."

"And I'm on the road a lot, preaching and speaking—I really need cruise control. And if you think about it, it's smarter to get some of the extras because the residual value is so much better (can you tell I did my homework?)." And on and on it went.

You're probably way ahead of me. I drove off the lot in a new pickup. Don't get me wrong—it was nice. I'd be lying if I said I didn't enjoy it. But it was way more than I needed. The truth is I just *wanted* the bells and whistles.

Your opinion of me is probably going to drop even more when I tell you this—it was only a few days into hunting season when I thought to myself, "You know, Hughes, you really should have gotten a four-wheel drive."

Do you struggle with a lack of contentment? Jesus didn't have a permanent place to lay his head, but he was content. He knew his heavenly Father would supply all his needs. He'll supply your needs as well—and probably a whole lot more.

"But godliness with contentment is great gain. For we brought nothing into the world, and we can take nothing out of it. But if we have food and clothing, we will be content with that" (1 Tim. 1:6–8).

How can you find that kind of contentment? Seek God's approval by having a thankful heart for all of his provisions. Here are some practical ways you can win the struggle with discontentment.

Focus on What You Have, Not on What You Don't Have

Parents, has this ever happened in your family? It's Christmas morning. Your children walk into the living room, rubbing the sleep out of their wide eyes. You try to have some sort of order as everyone begins opening presents, but after a while it's every person for himself or herself.

Before you know it, wrapping paper, ribbon, and bows are flying in all different directions. The mess reminds you of a scene in the movie Twister. Then, almost as quickly as the mayhem started, it's all over. A hush fills the room.

Finally, one of the little ones says what some of the others might be thinking but know better than to say out loud: "Is this all we get?"

We've seen the phenomenon of discontentment at my house during the evolution of the Nintendo video games systems. We purchased the first system for my sons (if you can remember back far enough, when it was just plain ole Nintendo).

After a few months, however, Super Nintendo was introduced. It had better graphics and better games. "But wait a second," we said. "You guys said this is the one you wanted. Remember? It's almost new." So our sons saved their money and got Super Nintendo. By this time we could see where this was headed.

They assured us they would be *completely* satisfied with the Super Nintendo system. They would *never* need or want another. This was it—right. It wasn't long before Nintendo 64 came along, with better graphics and better games—you know the rest of the spiel.

Isn't it frustrating as a parent when you don't feel like your child appreciates what you provide? I know you don't provide for them only to receive the thanks, but when they say thanks and demonstrate gratitude, you probably can't wait to do something else for them.

Now, let me ask you something. How do you think God feels when we aren't satisfied with what he provides? What is his reaction when we want bigger, fancier, faster, instead of being grateful for what he has given?

Oh, I know we tell him thanks. That's a good start. Our boys would say thanks, too. Then my wife and I would usually say, "We appreciate you guys telling us you are grateful. But we also want you to *show* us you're thankful, by being content with what you have." I think God would say the same thing to us.

Don't Measure Yourself by Someone Else's Standard of Living

Let's face it. Compared to most people in the world, we are rich. Most of us know where we're going to eat our next meal. Most of us will have a place to sleep tonight. Most of us have friends and family members who love us with all their hearts and would do anything for us. We're rich.

I was visiting a local tourist attraction near our home one day. As I walked in with my family, an elderly man was exiting the same area. He was wearing a cowboy hat and boots As he passed us he smiled at me. Then he said with a warm southern drawl, "Son, you are a rich man." He was so right.

We run into trouble with regard to contentment when we begin noticing what we don't have instead of what we have. We measure our prosperity by someone else's standard of living. The results are almost always destructive, because no matter how much you have, you can always find someone who has more.

I heard of a millionaire who was once asked, "How much money does a person need before he or she can say, 'That's enough'?" The millionaire answered, "One dollar more." Solomon wrote, "Whoever loves money never has money

106

enough; whoever loves wealth is never satisfied with his income. This too is meaningless" (Eccles. 5:10).

What's important is not that we are materially rich, but that we are spiritually rich because we have received the grace of God given through his Son. "In him we have redemption through his blood, the forgiveness of sins, in accordance with the riches of God's grace" (Eph. 1:7).

When Peter and John were going to the temple to pray, they passed a crippled beggar. The beggar asked the two men for the same thing he asked from everyone—money. Peter's answer to the man shows the abundance of our riches in Christ. He said, "Silver or gold I do not have, but what I have I give you. In the name of Jesus Christ of Nazareth, walk." And the man did just that.

Take Precautions If Necessary

Don't open yourself up to discontentment. If this is a problem area for you, stay away from the catalogs and advertisements that are designed to create a sense of dissatisfaction in the consumer. These temptations will only feed your discontentment. I've always heard that if you don't plan on going into the house, stay off the porch.

As you grow in your contentment and trust God to give you all that you need, you may not be as vulnerable. But when you are struggling, don't place yourself in a position to be discontent. Be honest about your vulnerability, and be on your guard.

Give Some Money or Possessions Away

Just as finding someone who has more than you is easy, locating people who have far less than you is simple too. Even though the following verses seem simplistic, they are still true: "It is more blessed to give than to receive" (Acts 20:35b), and "God loves a cheerful giver" (2 Cor. 9:7b).

As you give some things away, you will discover several lessons. You'll learn that some of those things you didn't think you could live without were dispensable after all. You'll discover the joy of realizing that God used you to meet the needs of another; in the same way he will use others to meet the need you have one day. And you will observe God blessing you by either replacing what you gave away or providing you with something else you need.

Tim St. Clair of Life Action Ministries shares what he calls "Living/Giving Principles" in crusades across America. One of the principles that has been meaningful to Page and me goes like this: God wants me to learn to give today out of my abundance (or supply), believing that tomorrow, if I have a need, God will use the abundance of others to meet my need (see 2 Cor. 8:13–15).

The concept of giving something up to meet the needs of another is nothing new. The first believers performed this act of benevolence. "All the believers were together and had everything in common. Selling their possessions and goods, they gave to anyone as he had need" (Acts 2:44–45).

I can't count the number of times I've been blessed by God through his people who lived by this principle. Just the other day (as a matter of fact, while I was working on this manuscript), I received a phone call from Page. She informed me how the Lord had given us a special gift.

The previous evening my mom, who lives eleven hours away in Louisville, Kentucky, had been in a serious car wreck. She was in intensive care. I knew she was in good hands, but I wanted to be with her nevertheless.

I called to check on the cost of flying to Louisville. It would be a quick trip, and I did not have the luxury of booking in advance, so the ticket was going to cost several hundred dollars. If flying was my only option, I would have had to pay the high price, but I didn't believe paying the high cost of the ticket was good stewardship, so I decided to drive.

I knew I wouldn't get there as quickly. I probably wouldn't be able to stay as long as I would like, but I would do my best.

Then I got the phone call from Page. I could sense her emotion in her voice. She had that "the Lord has done it again" sound in her voice.

She said she was holding in her hands an itinerary for Les Hughes, round trip to Louisville, Kentucky, from Jackson Mississippi. The ticket had been paid in full. As it turned out, some dear Christian friends learned of my desire to be with my mom, pooled their resources, and booked my flight for me.

Do I need to tell you who will be the first person to volunteer to meet a need the next time one is evident? You're right. Yours truly. And I guarantee I will jump at a chance to help any of those particular friends who ministered to me.

Contentment with Circumstances

As we've seen, seeking God's approval instead of attempting to impress people leads to contentment with your possessions. But that's not all. If our primary concern is to obey God and bloom where God plants us, we become content in our circumstances as well.

This is a lesson that has not come easily at all for me. I am a goal-driven person. That's not always bad, but if I'm not careful, I am unable to enjoy an accomplishment before I am running toward the next goal, pursuing the next challenge, or fighting the next giant.

Being content in your circumstances, good or bad, can be a hard pill to swallow. It's hard not to notice the greener grass on the other side of the fence. I once heard someone say, "The grass may be greener on the other side of the fence, but the water bill is probably a lot higher."

No position or circumstance is perfect. Different circumstances come with different sets of problems. We tend to overestimate the positive aspects of changing our circumstances and understate the positive things about our current set of circumstances.

In 1 Samuel 8, the Israelites told Samuel they were tired of being led by judges. They wanted a king. "They said to him,

'You are old, and your sons do not walk in your ways; now appoint a king to lead us, such as all the other nations have'" (1 Sam. 8:5).

Now there is a great reason to want a king: "We want to be like every other nation." Asking for an imperfect, human king was not a wise request. Instead of being content with God as the most perfect and just king, they wanted a flawed, human king like every other nation.

At first Samuel was offended by their request. He saw their desire for a king as a rejection of *his* leadership. God had a different perspective. The Lord said to Samuel, "It is not you they have rejected, but they have rejected me as their king" (1 Sam. 8:7).

God told Samuel he would honor the request of the people, but Samuel needed to warn the people first. A new king would tax the people in order to fill his coffers. A human king would send their sons to wage war on his enemies. A mortal king would use their family members, servants, crops, and livestock for his own benefit.

In spite of God's warnings, the people instructed Samuel to appoint a king. So God anointed Saul as the first king of Israel. There is a lesson here for you and me: Be careful what you ask God for. You just might get it.

At first Saul was a successful leader. But eventually he became arrogant and paranoid. Finally, he self-destructed. And he almost took the nation of Israel down with him.

There's nothing wrong with having lofty goals. Strive for excellence in whatever you do, but please be thankful to the Lord in all things. His purpose is being fulfilled in you, even when his timetable is not the same as yours.

Here's the key: keep your eyes on Jesus, not on your circumstances. On the Sea of Galilee, when Peter trusted in Jesus and looked at the Lord, he walked on water. When he took his eyes off Jesus and looked at his circumstances, namely the wind and the waves, he began to sink.

Fortunately for Peter, he was smart enough in his desperation to reach up and grab the hand of the Savior. Are you wise enough to do the same? Sometimes we have to sink a ways so that we will look up to him. You will never sink so low that you are out of the reach of God. Look up to him and take him by the hand. He will place your feet on solid ground.

On Christ the solid rock I stand,
All other ground is sinking sand.

It is a good day when we can say with the apostle Paul, "I have learned to be content whatever the circumstances. I know what it is to be in need, and I know what it is to have plenty. I have learned the secret of being content in any and every situation, whether well fed or hungry, whether living in plenty or in want. I can do everything through him who gives me strength" (Phil. 4:12–13).

Paul could write those words from a prison cell because he was living *above* his circumstances. He kept his eyes on the Lord. People could take away his possessions, but they could not take away the treasure of the gospel in his heart (see 2 Cor. 4:7). The government authorities could confiscate his property, but they could not seize his pearl of great price (see Matt. 13:45). The Roman officials could lock up his body, but they could not chain his spirit. He was free.

A Clear Conscience before God and Others

As we discussed previously, when a child of God seeks the approval of human beings instead of the approval of their heavenly Father, he or she will experience guilt as a result of disobedience. We can be grateful for the guilt, for at least two reasons.

First, the Holy Spirit makes us feel guilty so we will repent of our disobedience and turn to the Lord. Second, the next time we are facing a decision to be obedient to God or yield to human pressure, we will remember the pain of the guilt. Then we will be more likely to seek God's approval and not buckle under pressure.

Peter wrote, "But in your hearts set apart Christ as Lord. Always be prepared to give an answer to everyone who asks you to give the reason for the hope that you have. But do this with gentleness and respect, *keeping a clear conscience*, so that those who speak maliciously against your good behavior in Christ may be ashamed of their slander" (1 Pet. 3:15–16, emphasis mine).

When you seek God's approval, you should have no guilt. No regrets. You should have a crystal-clear conscience that you've done the right thing. That's why Paul could say with joy in his heart, "Rejoice in the Lord always. I will say it again: Rejoice! Let your gentleness be evident to all. The Lord is near. Do not be anxious about anything, but in everything, by prayer and petition, with thanksgiving, present your requests to God. And the *peace of God*, which transcends all understanding, will guard your hearts and your minds in Christ Jesus" (Phil. 4:4–7, emphasis mine).

People go to great lengths in our day to have a clear conscience. But there is only one way to have real contentment and peace: respond to the Lord's tugging at your heart. Look to him and take him by the hand. When someone is born anew into God's family, there is only one way to live in peace and contentment: Seek his favor more that the approval of human beings.

Personal Revival

"If my people, who are called by my name, will humble themselves and pray and seek my face and turn from their wicked ways, then I will hear from heaven and will forgive their sin and will heal their land" (2 Chron. 7:14).

Another positive result of living for the approval of the Father is a spiritual revival in the life of his child. Now, please hear me. I'm not one of these folks who is always looking for the next spiritual high. I know people, as you do I'm sure, who are always looking for that ecstatic worship experience, or tape, or book, to meet some kind of emotional need. That's not what I'm referring to.

God is just as present and real in the valley as he is on the mountaintop. In fact, most of life is lived off of the mountain. But when you and I are obedient to him, he will allow us periodic fresh encounters with him that cannot be supplied by all the human applause in the world. "Though I walk in the midst of trouble, Thou wilt revive me; Thou wilt stretch forth Thy hand against the wrath of my enemies, And Thy right hand will save me" (Ps. 138:7, NASB).

Overseeing a construction project doesn't sound like a glamorous line of work, but that was the task given to Nehemiah by God. Talk about a non–mountaintop experience. Nehemiah's call to do God's will did not come out of an emotional worship experience like the call of Isaiah. When God called Nehemiah to go to Jerusalem, the city had been destroyed. But God gave Nehemiah a burden for his people.

Nehemiah was the cupbearer of Artaxerxes, king of Persia. The cupbearer was the person who tasted the wine, and probably the food, of the king. The cupbearer was more expendable than the king. If someone attempted to poison the king, the poison didn't go any further than the cupbearer. Of course, the cupbearer didn't go any further than the poison either.

This frequent access to the king led to a special relationship between the two men. The relationship also potentially gave Nehemiah a lot of influence.

Nehemiah was a Jewish man living in Persia as a result of the fall of Jerusalem in 587 B.C. Thousands of Jews were subsequently exiled. When we meet Nehemiah in the Scriptures, the year is about 446 B.C. The time of year is between mid-November and mid-December.

Nehemiah received discouraging news concerning those who were still in Jerusalem after the exile: "They said to me, 'Those who survived the exile and are back in the province are in great trouble and disgrace. The wall of Jerusalem is broken down, and its gates have been burned with fire'" (Neh. 1:3). The discouraged cupbearer added, "When I heard these things, I sat down and wept. For some days I mourned and fasted and prayed before the God of heaven" (Neh. 1:4).

Nehemiah had bottomed out—to the extent that even the king noticed and asked, "Why does your face look so sad when you are not ill? This can be nothing but sadness of heart" (Neh. 2:2). But God spoke to Nehemiah in the valley.

In all the chaos and turmoil of knowing the state of his homeland, Nehemiah wisely turned to God and asked for the Father's favor. He entreated the Lord, "O Lord, let your ear be attentive to the prayer of this your servant and to the prayer of your servants who delight in revering your name. Give your servant success today by granting him favor in the presence of this man" (Neh. 1:11).

Nehemiah eventually went to the king to ask for his favor (see Neh. 2:5), but he knew without God's approval his work would fail. The job of rebuilding the wall of Jerusalem was what Henry Blackaby called a "God-sized task."

Nehemiah made several requests of Artaxerxes—an extended leave of absence, letters of transit, requisitions for timber to build the city gates—and the king granted every request. Still, Nehemiah was careful to give credit for the success of the project to whom credit was due: "And because the gracious hand of my God was upon me, the king granted my requests" (Neh. 2:8b)—not because the king was benevolent, not because Nehemiah gave a convincing appeal, but because the cupbearer had the approval of his heavenly Father.

The wall was completed in excellent time—fifty-two days to be precise—and God was glorified. But the physical protection of the people, the temple, and their city was not the only result of the faithfulness of God's servant. Remember, we're talking revival here.

When the people saw God's hand at work and the critics of the work silenced, they experienced a spiritual renewal. Chapter

10 says the people took an oath "to follow the Law of God given through Moses the servant of God and to obey carefully all the commands, regulations and decrees of the LORD our Lord" (v. 29b).

Nehemiah, along with Ezra, helped bring back to Judah a love for the Word of God. The two men led in a celebration and thanksgiving service for the Lord's blessing. Large choirs came together. "And on that day they offered great sacrifices, rejoicing because God had given them great joy. The women and children also rejoiced. The sound of rejoicing in Jerusalem could be heard far away" (Neh. 12:43). No P.A. system was needed.

The book of Nehemiah ends by sharing the heart of the cupbearer with the reader. Really, Nehemiah's desire was not different at the end of the book than at the beginning. At the beginning of the book, Nehemiah was discouraged, but basically he wanted one thing: the favor, the approval, the applause of God. And so the book ends with the same request. "Remember me with favor, O my God" (Neh. 13:31).

What more could we hope for? When we have God's approval nothing else matters. When we have God's favor, we will experience revival. And so will many around us. Revival is contagious. Like many around Nehemiah were influenced by his faithfulness, people around you will be influenced by your obedience to the Lord.

I mentioned the experience of worship that resulted from Nehemiah's seeking God's favor. Let's look at this result in a little more detail as it took place in the life of another who sought the approval of God.

Freedom in Worship

In Scripture, many terms are used to describe people who seek God's approval. In 1 Samuel, David is called "a man after God's own heart" (see 1 Sam. 13:14). He wasn't perfect. Far from it. His sins and shortcomings have been the subject matter for many sermons and Bible studies.

We can identify with David. He wanted so desperately to be a man after God's own heart, but he constantly struggled with the flesh. Yet even when David failed, he turned to God in humility, begging the Lord to restore the joy of his salvation.

An event in the life of David illustrates how seeking God's approval can lead to freedom in worship. The event is David's bringing back the ark of the covenant to Jerusalem. This story can serve as a good example to God's people who long for fresh experiences with God in worship.

As I go to different churches and speak to church leaders, I am noticing a real hunger for meaningful worship. People are weary of being able to predict what will happen when they come to God's house. They are looking for the same sense of God's presence in corporate worship as was present among God's people in the Bible. More and more persons are wanting to say, "I've experienced worship," not "I've been to church."

The story of David's success in bringing the ark of the covenant back to Jerusalem is recorded in 2 Samuel 6. The ark was a chest, laden with gold. It contained the staff of Aaron, the brother of Moses; a jar of manna, the food provided by God to the Hebrew people as they journeyed to the promised land; and the stone tablets of the covenant.

David's first attempt to bring the ark back to where it belonged was unsuccessful (2 Sam. 6:1–7). One man lost his life because the ark was not treated with proper reverence.

So David tried again. On his second attempt, David was successful. When the people brought the ark into the city of Jerusalem, David's joy was so great he could not contain himself. He danced before the Lord "with all his might" (2 Sam. 6:14).

Now what in the world would cause the king of a nation to undress partially and to dance—right out in public? He danced before family, friends, priests, community leaders, and even his own servants. Doesn't sound like something a dignified king would do, does it?

Well, to understand David's ecstasy, we need to know the religious significance of the ark. (This is a little side road, but it will help us appreciate the story better). The most important thing about the ark was not what it contained, but what it represented: the presence of Almighty God. The ark's rightful place was the Holy of Holies, the most sacred part of the Old Testament tabernacle.

The Holy of Holies could be entered only by the high priest on one day of the year, the Day of Atonement. The high priest went through a process of purification so as not to stand defiled in the presence of Almighty God. Then the high priest would offer a sacrifice to God on his own behalf and to acknowledge the sins of his people.

On the top cover of the ark, called the mercy seat, were two gold cherubim, or winged creatures, facing one another. The High Priest would take the blood of the animals he had sacrificed and sprinkled some of the blood on the mercy seat. On this mercy seat, God met with his people (Exod. 25:22).

This ark, the meeting place between a holy God and sinful human beings, had been in the hands of David's enemies, the Philistines. That explains why David was overjoyed to see the ark entering the holy city of Jerusalem. In reality, God had not left the people of Israel literally, but the ark played a central role in their religion. For all intents and purposes, as far as the people of Israel were concerned, the absence of the ark was equivalent to God's blessing being taken away. Can you imagine the sense of emptiness they must have felt?

So David's demonstrative reaction makes sense after all, doesn't it? But David's joy wasn't shared by everyone. Someone in the story believed the king should be above such undignified displays of emotion. Her name was Michal. She was the daughter of Saul, David's predecessor. She also happened to be David's wife.

Michal watched as her husband danced before his subjects and stated (I assume sarcastically), "How the king of Israel has distinguished himself today" (2 Sam. 6:20b).

Wouldn't that criticism have stung you a little? We don't know precisely what was going on in David's heart, but his response was classic: "It was before the LORD, who chose me rather than your father or anyone from his house when he appointed me ruler over the LORD's people Israel—I will celebrate before the LORD. I will become even more undigified than this, and I will be humiliated in my own eyes" (2 Sam. 6:21–22).

The king was not attempting to win the approval even of his own wife. His purpose was to express thanks to God. He was overwhelmed with the return of God's blessing to the people of Israel. The king couldn't contain his emotions. Expressive worship tends to be undignified.

David probably would have welcomed gladly Michal's joining him in this celebration and expression of worship. She chose instead to be critical of his experience. But he didn't let her cynicism and criticism throw a wet blanket on his experience.

David was perceptive. He understood that her criticism of him actually didn't have anything to do with his dance. Her actions had everything to do with what was inside of her, namely bitterness. God had anointed her father, Saul, as the first king of Israel. Saul began well, but his disobedience to the Lord eventually led to his downfall, and God chose another to lead his people. He chose David.

Saul's influence began to fade away. David's grew. Finally, the people of Israel created a catchy ditty. They sang, "Saul has slain his thousands, and David his tens of thousands," a refrain that galled her father, Saul (see 1 Sam. 18:7–8).

David's confidence grew with his success. Saul on the other hand, became paranoid and desperate. In a devastating battle with the Philistines, King Saul deliberately fell on his own sword and took his life.

Saul's bitterness and jealousy of David evidently still lived through his daughter Michal. The contents of her heart eventually came out of her mouth through her comments about her husband's public display. David, however, did not allow her to take away his joy or the experience.

Now what about you and me? What does this story have to do with how seeking God's approval leads to freedom in worship? Well, first of all, please understand that God has created us as people who long for worship.

Remember how our journey to understand our need for approval began? Where did our approval drive come from? It came from the Lord himself. He gave it to us so we would seek his approval. People possess a longing to worship. And we *will* fill this longing to worship with someone or something.

This need for genuine expressions of worship is being fulfilled in some rather traditional institutions. There is a growing sense of God's Holy Spirit at work in corporate worship—in churches, on seminary and Bible college campuses, and on campuses of state and private universities.

Recently at Mississippi College (MC), where I serve on faculty, we had an unusual chapel service where this phenomenon was demonstrated. The worship service was one of the last chapels of the year. Our chapel services are compulsory, and frankly the students aren't always excited about being there. To tell you the truth, humanly speaking, there was nothing special about this particular chapel. A student spoke and did a fine job, but we had heard good chapel speakers before.

Something was different about that particular worship experience, however. A noticeable spiritual dynamic was present. By the end of the service, the Holy Spirit had taken center stage.

An invitation was given at the end of the service, and hundreds of students flooded the aisles of the auditorium and made their way to the front. Many people fell to their knees in humble confession before the Lord. Pockets of prayer groups formed around the auditorium as young men and women poured out their hearts to God and to one another.

A lot of healing took place that day, both on a vertical and a horizontal level. The chapel time, normally about thirty minutes, went well into the next class period that Tuesday, but not many people complained.

What happened? People responded to the moving of the Holy Spirit. That's the only way to explain it. At the same time this was happening at MC, at least two other churches in our state were having similar experiences. These were not "charismatic" churches, at least not in the sense that the term is used normally.

The need to express ourselves in corporate worship is one of the reasons for the success of the Promise Keepers movement. Men from various church and cultural backgrounds are experiencing expressive, meaningful worship (some for the first time) and feeling less inhibited concerning their praise for God. The conferences provide an atmosphere where demonstrative worship is accepted and encouraged.

I am not saying physically demonstrative worship is the only legitimate way to express our honor, thanks, and devotion to God. I know people who worship the Lord on a deep, cerebral level. For them, meaningful worship is not a flood of emotions or feelings, but a stream of thought and understanding.

No one form of worship is ever mandated in Scripture as the only acceptable or pleasing form to God. Jesus said those who worship God must worship him in spirit and in truth. If a form of worship does not go contrary to the teachings of Scripture, is honoring to the Lord, and brings glory to him and not other human beings, then don't be afraid to express it.

Recently, my wife and several members of our church family attended a revival meeting at a nearby church. Most, if not all, of the members of that church, St. Mark's Missionary Baptist Church, are African American.

Our pastor, Hal Kitchings, is close friends with the pastor of St. Mark's, Dennis Grant. Dennis asked Hal to be the revival preacher. Our choir, including my wife, Page, sang during the services. I missed the services at St. Mark's because of speaking engagements and other commitments, but I couldn't wait to get home every night and hear what had happened in the services.

New brothers and sisters in Christ formed a fresh appreciation for the similarities and the differences between the congregations and their styles of worship. The week probably affected the folks of Morrison Heights Baptist Church (my church family) more than the members of St. Mark's.

Morrison Heights has a reputation of having a more contemporary style of worship compared to congregations with more traditional or liturgical styles. Compared to St. Mark's worship, however, Morrison Heights was formal. During the preaching, one African-American woman would raise her hand in the air and say, "Well." Another would say calmly, "Lord, Lord." My favorite was "Fix it, Preacher!"

It didn't take long for the members of Morrison Heights to loosen up. Pretty soon they were taking part in the services in a more demonstrative way. I even heard someone in the Morrison Heights choir said, "Fix it, Preacher" during the first Sunday service they were back home. What happened? They felt more freedom in worship because they weren't concerned with what people around them thought. They realized God was their audience.

No one type of worship is necessarily right or wrong. Scripture refers to being still and knowing that he is God; raising holy hands unto the Lord; clapping our hands; shouting for joy; falling on our faces before God; bending our knees; bowing our heads; lifting our faces to the heavens; and many other forms of worship.

Those whose worship is more demonstrative should not be condemned for "putting on a show." And people whose worship is more reserved and solemn must not be accused of being "less spiritual." Only God knows the heart. I also must remember that just because something makes me uncomfortable does not mean it is not pleasing in the sight of God.

With regard to our worship, it's helpful to focus less on the means and more on our role compared to God's role in worship. Some people enter worship as if the worship leader, minister, or singers are the performers, God is the conductor, and the people are the audience. That model does not have a biblical precedent.

The biblical model of worship is that we are the participants (performers if you will, although I don't care much for the term), the worship leader is both participant and prompter, and God is our audience. Worship is *to* him and *for* him.

Jesus said, "True worshipers will worship *the Father*" (John 4:23b, emphasis mine). He is the object of our worship. Worship is for his pleasure, not ours. Our pleasure comes from knowing we've been obedient to him, that we have his approval.

Now let's go back to David and the ark (don't let me lose you, now. This is the most important part). You and I have a greater reason to dance (figuratively speaking, of course) or to celebrate than David did. Our reason for celebration is based on eternal matters of much more importance than the ark.

In addition to the information in the Old Testament about the ark of the covenant, the New Testament mentions the ark of the covenant and its mercy seat as well. The Greek word *hilasterion* means "mercy seat," the cover on the ark (see Heb. 9:5)—the meeting place between people and God. In Romans 3:25 the apostle Paul referred to Jesus as God's propitiation, or sacrifice of atonement, expiation, depending on the translation you read.

Guess what word Paul used in Romans 3:25 to describe God's act of mercy through the blood Jesus shed on the cross? You guessed it—*hilasterion*. In other words, Jesus is our mercy seat. He is the meeting place between a holy God and sinful people, where mercy takes place. He is the place where we meet God.

As a matter of fact, the writer of Hebrews explains that the experience of the people in the Old Testament regarding the sacrifical system and the ark of the covenant was only a *shadow* of the real thing. Please look at it in the author's own words:

> When Christ came as high priest of the good things that are already here, he went through the greater and more perfect tabernacle that is not man-made, that is to say, not a part of this creation. He did not enter by means of the blood of goats and calves; but he entered the Most Holy Place once for all by his own blood, having obtained eternal redemption. The blood of goats and bulls and the ashes of a heifer sprinkled on those who are ceremonially unclean sanctify them so that they are outwardly clean. How much more, then, will the blood of Christ, who through the eternal Spirit offered himself unblemished to God, cleanse our consciences from acts that lead to death, so that we may serve the living God! (Heb. 9:11–14)

Jesus was and is the real high priest. He didn't need to go through the normal ritualistic cleansing the flawed high priest went through. He was perfect. He was the only one truly qualified to enter the presence of the Father on behalf of sinful people.

> For Christ did not enter a man-made sanctuary that was only a copy of the true one; he entered heaven itself, now to appear for us in God's presence. Nor did he enter heaven to offer himself again and again, the way the high priest enters the Most Holy Place every year with blood that is not his own. Then Christ would have had to suffer many times since the creation of the world. But now he has appeared once for all at the end of the ages to do away with sin by the sacrifice of himself. Just as man is destined to die once, and after that to face judgment, so Christ was sacrificed once to take away the sins of many people; and he will appear a second time, not to bear sin, but to bring salvation to those who are waiting for him. (Heb. 9:24-28)

Jesus did not enter a tent made with human hands. He entered heaven, a city whose builder and maker is God. And he entered only once. That was enough. The Old Testament high priest entered the Holy of Holies in the tabernacle on the Day of Atonement every year. Sounds futile, doesn't it?

Look at how the author of Hebrews compared the futility of the Old Testament sacrificial system to the finality of God's work through Jesus on the cross: "Day after day every priest stands and performs his religious duties; again and again he offers the same sacrifices, which can never take away sins. But when this priest had offered for all time one sacrifice for sins, he sat down at the right hand of God" (Heb. 10:11–12).

John wrote that Jesus is our advocate with the Father. "My little children, I am writing these things to you that you may not sin. And if anyone sins, we have an Advocate with the Father, Jesus Christ the righteous; and He Himself is the propitiation for our sins; and not for ours only, but also for those of the whole world" (1 John 2:1-2, NASB).

When Jesus said "It is finished" from the cross, he wasn't referring to his life. He was referring to his divine task to take away the sins of the world. He completed his mission and sat down at the right hand of the Father.

Consider Charles Wesley's hymn, "Arise, My Soul, Arise":

> *He ever lives above*
> *For me to intercede,*
> *His all-redeeming love,*
> *His precious blood, to plead;*
> *His blood atoned for all our race,*
> *And sprinkles now the throne of grace.*
> *Five bleeding wounds He bears,*
> *Received on Calvary;*
> *They pour effectual prayers,*
> *They strongly speak for me;*
> *Forgive him, O forgive! they cry,*
> *Nor let the ransom'd sinner die!*

That's something to shout about, isn't it? I wonder what King David would do if he were to live on this side of Calvary. He reacted to the sight of the ark of the covenant by dancing. It was a beautiful sight to him. But it had limitations. It could be stolen by human beings. Even today, no one is certain of its whereabouts. When we experience the blessing of God's forgiveness through his Son, Jesus, our hearts should dance.

In God's saving work through Jesus on the cross, he provided something that cannot be taken away. It can't be kidnapped. It won't decay or wear out. It never becomes obsolete. His salvation is forever—once and for all.

"For I am convinced that neither death nor life, neither angels nor demons, neither the present nor the future, nor any powers, neither height nor depth, nor anything else in all creation, will be able to separate us from the love of God that is in Christ Jesus our Lord" (Rom. 8:38–39).

When you and I learn this truth and truly experience his salvation, our reaction should be similar to David's. Why be concerned about our reputation, or our dignity, or appearing undistinguished before people? Our only concern is that we offer our heavenly Father the worship of which he is worthy. That we draw attention to him not to ourselves. That we worship him in spirit and in truth.

And when we acknowledge that Jesus is our mercy seat—where mercy takes place, where God reaches his hand down to us—how shall we respond?

How else? Our hearts will dance!

Racial Reconciliation

I know I don't need to convince you of the need for racial reconciliation in our nation and in our world—between Caucasians and African Americans, Jews and Arabs, Hispanics and Asians. Even as I write these words, the governments of India and Pakistan are taking turns showing their military might to one another by detonating nuclear devices. Apart from a miracle, these situations seems hopeless.

Governments haven't offered lasting solutions. Peace treaties have been broken. Summits between officials rarely lead to permanent positive results. Sensitivity training and education have not stamped out prejudice. All of our human effort has only seemed to make matters more tense. What's the solution?

I'm not trying to be simplistic. I realize the complexity of these matters. The roots of these issues go back hundreds, in some cases, thousands, of years. But please hear me out for just a few moments and consider how seeking God's approval instead of human applause can lead to racial reconciliation.

If you ever have an opportunity, observe small children of different skin colors who have been placed in a setting together. Most of the time they will play and interact without any concern for their differences. They aren't blind; their differences in hue simply don't matter to them.

But if a child in a group of older children begins putting pressure on those having the same skin color to be separated from others who are different, often they will join those like themselves because they are concerned over what others will think of them. Some people never grow out of that fear. There's a line in the movie *West Side Story* that says, "You've got to be taught to hate."

To illustrate this point, I want to share with you the pilgrimage (sort of a God-initiated sensitivity training) of a man who struggled with prejudice in part because of his fear of what others would think of him. His name was Simon Peter.

Wait a minute. Are we talking about the same Simon Peter who made the inspired confession, "You are the Christ, the Son of the living God?" That's the one. Is this the same Peter who drew a sword and tried to split the skull of the high priest's servant in the garden of Gethsemane for arresting Jesus? One and the same. The same Peter who stood boldly before the religious officials and said, "Judge for yourselves whether it is right in God's sight to obey you rather than God. For we cannot help speaking about what we have seen and heard" (Acts 4:19–20)? That's him.

Old Attitudes Die Hard

Simon Peter was changed radically after the resurrection. The transformation he experienced in Christ allowed him to take

126

huge steps in being freed from the bondage of the opinion of others. Before the resurrection, he was afraid to tell a slave girl he was a follower of Jesus (see Matt. 26:69–70).

After the resurrection of Jesus and at the end of his life, tradition has it that Peter requested to the authorities to be crucified upside down. He did not consider himself worthy to die in the same manner as the Lord Jesus. What courage.

After that resurrection Sunday morning, Peter was not as concerned with what antagonists of the gospel thought about him as he had been before. But he dragged his feet when it came to what *religious* people thought about him—people who were just like him in many ways. Peter wanted their approval, even though some of their traditions and beliefs went contrary to God's instructions.

The prejudice shown by some of the Jewish people of antiquity had religious roots. God commanded his people to be distinct from the rest of the nations of the world. The other nations worshipped idols and pagan gods. The God of Abraham, Isaac, and Jacob was a jealous God and wanted the full allegiance of his creation.

The ancient Jews saw themselves as distinct, holy people. The non-Jews were considered unholy, unclean, and in some cases, even less than human. Peter shared this view. One of the reasons Jesus came was to change that perception and to break down the walls of prejudice that people had erected.

With all the progress Peter made as his faith matured, his need for the approval of people still manifested itself in prejudice toward the Gentiles. In the book of Acts, Luke told how God changed Peter's heart regarding the Gentiles. Paul later told how Peter needed honest confrontation from a brother in Christ (see Galatians 2).[2] I'd like briefly to examine Luke's account in Acts in order to see the transformation that took place in Peter's life.

Peter's Struggle with Prejudice

Luke described the important event in Acts 10 and 11. He introduced a Gentile soldier named Cornelius who lived in Caesarea. Cornelius himself was seeking the approval of the same God Simon Peter served. He worshipped the God of Israel by giving to the poor and praying daily (by the way, these are two of the three expressions of religion discussed by Jesus in the Sermon on the Mount). This man Cornelius was on the right track regarding his relationship with God.

An angel of God appeared to Cornelius and told him God had received his prayers and offerings. The angel instructed Cornelius to send for a man named Simon Peter, who was in the city of Joppa at the home of Simon the tanner.

The following day, even as the men sent by Cornelius were on their way to Joppa, God spoke to Peter through a vision. While Peter was praying on the roof of his host's house, he fell into a trance. He saw heaven open and something like a large sheet came down from heaven.

On the sheet Peter observed all kinds of animals—even some that were considered unclean by Jewish people. A voice told Peter to "Get up, Peter. Kill and eat" (Acts 10:13). Peter answered, "Surely not, Lord! . . . I have never eaten anything impure or unclean" (10:14).

The voice answered, "What God has cleansed, no longer consider unholy" (10:15, NASB). This happened three times in the vision, and the sheet was taken back up to heaven. While Peter was pondering the vision, the men sent by Cornelius arrived at the house where Peter was staying.

The men explained the reasons Cornelius had sent them. The next day Peter accompanied the men back to the home of Cornelius in Caesarea. By the time Peter arrived at the home of the Gentile family, he had made sense of the rooftop vision.

Peter's Change of Heart

The first sign Peter's heart was changing was his willingness to go into the home of the centurion. Peter said to the people in the house, "You are well aware that it is against our law for a Jew to associate with a Gentile or visit him. But God has shown me that I should not call any man impure or unclean" (Acts 10:28).

The second indication of Peter's transformation was his response to the centurion and his family. Cornelius related to Peter the details of his angelic vision, and Peter knew why God had sent him. This Gentile needed to hear the good news about Jesus. Luke explained, "Then Peter began to speak: 'I now realize how true it is that God does not show favoritism but accepts men from every nation who fear him and do what is right'" (Acts 10:34–35).

Luke then explained how Cornelius and his household were saved, received the gift of the Holy Spirit, and were baptized. The result of this event was victory for the members of Cornelius' household, but the ordeal wasn't over yet for Peter. He still had to go back to the Jewish Christians in Jerusalem and explain why he had gone into the house of "uncircumcised men" (see Acts 11:1–4).

Peter retold the story to the Jerusalem Christians. Six other Christian brothers who had gone to the centurion's home with Peter supported his story. After giving an account of the previous few days, Peter concluded, "As I began to speak, the Holy Spirit came on them as he had come on us at the beginning. Then I remembered what the Lord had said: 'John baptized with water, but you will be baptized with the Holy Spirit.' So if God gave them the same gift as he gave us, who believed in the Lord Jesus Christ, *who was I to think that I could oppose God*? (Acts 11:15-17, emphasis mine).

After Peter's convincing and passionate testimony, and the corroboration of the other witness, the formerly skeptical Jerusalem leaders had no further objections. They praised God for what he had done, saying, "So then, God has granted even the Gentiles repentance unto life" (Acts 11:18b).

Later, in Galatians 2:11, this issue troubled Peter again. Fortunately for Peter, Paul loved him enough to confront him about it. Peter was wrong to care more about pleasing fellow Jews than pleasing God. Paul was motivated to confront Peter by his dedication to truth. In the apostle's words, those who would not accept the Gentiles on God's terms were "not acting in line with the truth of the gospel" (Gal. 2:14).

Results of Reconciliation

As a result of God's prompting Peter, and Paul's rebuking him, Peter was liberated from the fear of man in this area of prejudice. Peter overcame his prejudice and concern of what others thought and did the right thing. "The Lord's hand was with them, and a great number of people believed and turned to the Lord" (Acts 11:21).

What about you and me? Does our concern over what others think keep us from having relationships with brothers and sisters in Christ whose skin is a different color from ours? How open are we to people of different hues worshipping with us or becoming members of the church we attend?

Governments haven't been able to reconcile people. Education hasn't done it. The entertainment industry hasn't been successful. If you think about it for a moment, the places on our globe that are having a positive impact on bringing people together are successful because they are motivated by a common faith in Christ.

I've mentioned the partnership formed by the Morrison Heights and St. Mark's churches. They represent only a fraction of the hundreds of churches who are tired of the fighting. Instead of shooting at one another, these and many like them are dedicating themselves to making a difference for Jesus and reaching their communities for Christ.

The Imperials used to sing a song that included the line, "There will never be any peace until God is seated at the conference table." If we refuse to be influenced by what others might think; if we seek to please God and be obedient to him only; if we agree with God that we are all equal in his eyes; then we can agree with Paul: "There is *one* body and *one* Spirit—just as you were called to *one* hope when you were called—*one* Lord, *one* faith, *one* baptism; *one* God and Father of all, who is over all and through all and in all" (Eph. 4:4–6, emphasis mine).

If God Is Our Father . . .

If God is our Father, any Christian is your brother or sister. Just imagine what could happen if the body of Christ would lock arms and do battle with Satan and be unified in our efforts to share the gospel of Jesus Christ with the world. I saw this kind of unity demonstrated once, and I've never been the same since. The event occurred at the Promise Keeper's Clergy Conference in Atlanta, Georgia.

Whether you agree theologically or philosophically with "the seven principles of a promise keeper," one thing is for certain— the leaders of this movement have worked hard to reconcile people of different color and denominational backgrounds. I'll never forget the sight of thousands of Christian men of all colors and denominations embracing as they asked God and one another for forgiveness of prejudice and hatred—big burly men with tears streaming down their face, smiling for joy because of the weight lifted off of their shoulders.

What liberation they experienced—Native American, African American, Asian American, Hispanic American, Caucasian, Jew, and Gentile—all were one in Christ Jesus. Then Steve Green, along with a one-hundred-voice male choir, sang these words:

Let the walls fall down.
Let the walls fall down.
Let the walls that divide us
and hide us fall down.

If in Christ we agree,
Let us seek unity.
Let the walls, let the walls fall down.[3]

Steve Green's appearance reflected the anointing of God that night. I know this sounds crazy, but it was almost as if his face was glowing as he sang that song from the bottom of his heart.

Brothers and sisters in Christ, the world has not seen what can happen if the church of Jesus Christ would unite against evil with the same intensity as we have sometimes fought against one another. Wouldn't it be great to leave that kind of spiritual legacy to our sons and daughters and grandchildren? We can turn the tide. Will you do it?

This was beautifully demonstrated by the truly special participants in the Special Olympics. One year, runners lined up to run the one-hundred-yard dash. When the gun sounded, eight athletes bolted toward the finish line. Observers said at first all you could see were arms and legs.

Then about halfway through the race, one of the leaders tripped over his own feet and fell hard to the ground. That's when something extraordinary took place. All the other runners stopped. They picked up their fallen colleague, brushed him off, locked arms, and walked arm in arm across the finish line together.

What a great example for the church. We aren't competitors. We are called to be one. We're called to build one another up. When one falls, the others lend support. When one is hurt, we are to pick him or her up. Then we can walk across the finish line together.

"There is neither Jew nor Greek, slave nor free, male nor female, for you are all one in Christ Jesus" (Gal. 3:28).

Godly Courage

"The wicked man flees though no one pursues, but the righteous are as bold as a lion" (Prov. 28:1).

Another result of overcoming the fear of man is supernatural courage and boldness. If you fear another human being, that fear did not come from God. Notice what Paul told his son in the faith, Timothy: "For God has not given us a spirit of timidity, but of power and love and discipline. Therefore do not be ashamed of the testimony of our Lord . . ." (2 Tim. 1:7–8a, NASB).

Mike Gilchrist has preached boldly the gospel of Jesus Christ for about forty years. He's still going strong. I can remember Mike preaching revivals in churches where my family worshipped when I was a little boy. Now he is my colleague and brother in ministry, and I still look up to him because of his courage and faithfulness through the years.

Mike preached a revival meeting for us while I served First Baptist Church in Summit, Mississippi. I'll never forget a story he told during one of the worship services. Mike was able to survive a perilous situation in part because he did not fear a man who threatened his life.

One quiet Saturday morning, Mike was leaving a post office near his home when he came face-to-face with a man pointing a gun at him. The man demanded that Mike give him all his money, anything of value, and the keys to Mike's car.

Now to appreciate fully the story you should know that Mike Gilchrist is a giant in the pulpit, but physically small of stature. He stands about 5' 8" and weighs about 150 pounds ringing wet. He has snow-white hair and the heart of a lion.

He looked at the man who was holding the gun in the eyes. Knowing the thief could pull the trigger at any moment, Mike said, "Young man, when I was sixteen years old Jesus saved me. Right then I gave my life and everything I had and ever will have to the Lord Jesus Christ. He owns it all."

Then Mike took the money out of his pockets and put it on the counter in the post office lobby, and said, "There's Jesus' money." He did the same with his watch and said, "There's his watch." He laid his keys on the counter and said, "And there are his car keys."

The armed man froze with his mouth open and eyes fixed on Mike, as if he didn't know what to say or do. Then the thief looked down at the money, and back up at Mike, and finally glanced at the money one more time. Suddenly he grabbed the money and ran. My friend trusted in the name of the Lord Jesus Christ more than he did another human being.

Mike said that after the event he felt rather violated, but while it was taking place he had absolute peace—no fear. In fact, when Mike saw the man flee the scene on foot and realized he only wanted the car keys so Mike wouldn't chase after him, he yelled out at the thief to throw his keys in nearby tall grass (later, he realized that was probably not a wise thing to do). But the man ignored Mike and ran away. What gave the preacher so much boldness? Mike knew the worse thing the man could do to him was to end a wonderful life on earth that had been fruitful for the Lord. But God intervened, and the bandit unwittingly added to Mike's testimony of how God has been faithful through the years.

You might say, "Yeah, that's fine for your friend, but what about those who aren't as fortunate? What if the gunman had pulled the trigger? The story wouldn't have such a happy ending then, would it? I had a loved one who was murdered, [or brutalized, or beaten, or abused, or raped]. What about her?"

Humanly speaking, you're right. Things don't always turn out the way they did for my friend Mike. People all around us live in fear because they have loved ones who have suffered at the hands of another. Some live in fear because of their surroundings or daily circumstances.

God doesn't always intervene the way we hope and pray he will. Still, you can be assured of this: God is faithful and will be glorified in the life and in the death of his children.

Jack Vincent was a missionary in China who had an experience like Mike Gilchrist's, but with drastically different results.

Jack was robbed at gunpoint by a Chinese bandit. The robber put a gun to Jack's head and said, "Are you afraid? I'm going to kill you." Jack Vincent responded, "Afraid? Of what? I'd just go right to be with God." The gunman pulled the trigger and killed the missionary.

E. H. Hamilton, a fellow missionary, learned about the tragedy and wrote this poem:

> *Afraid, of what?*
> *To feel the Spirit's glad release?*
> *To pass from pain to perfect peace?*
> *The strife and strain of life to cease?*
> *Afraid? Of that?*
> *Afraid? Of what?*
> *Afraid to see the Savior's face?*
> *To hear his welcome and to trace*
> *The glory gleaned from wounds of grace?*
> *Afraid? Of that?*
> *Afraid? Of what?*
> *To enter into heaven's rest?*
> *And yet to serve the Master's blest.*
> *From service good to service best?*
> *Afraid? Of that?*[4]

Please try to be honest with yourself. Is there a person or persons in your life of whom you are afraid? An employer or superior at work? A spouse? A person at school? Someone at the church who intimidates you? Maybe even your own child?

If any person poses a physical threat to you, you are wise to pray for God to provide you a way to safety, and then to take action when he provides the opportunity. But if you have placed your life into the hands of God, you have no reason to live in fear.

"Have no fear of sudden disaster or of the ruin that overtakes the wicked, for the LORD will be your confidence and will keep your foot from being snared" (Prov. 3:25–26).

When our youngest son was four and our daughter (known as the "empress of the universe" at our house) was two, Page took them to get some shots they were due. We've been blessed in that, for the most part, our children have been healthy, so they were strangers to the surroundings of the doctor's office.

Page sensed their uneasiness and watched as their big brown eyes panned the room. Then the empress broke the silence with a song. The chorus she sang was a prayer she had learned, based on Psalm 56:3–4 and went like this:

> *When I am afraid, I will trust in You.*
> *I will trust in You; I will trust in You.*
> *When I am afraid, I will trust in You.*
> *In God whose word I praise.*[5]

After my daughter began the tune, my son, Luke, joined in. There they were in the office with the coughing and sneezing adults, comforting one another with the presence of God and his promise to calm our fears. Out of the mouths of babes.

Singing the little tune was their way of saying, "I'm afraid, Lord. But I trust you. I believe you are still in control. Everything's going to be OK." And it was. Oh, by the way—the tune did wonders for their mom, too.

Some of our fears are rather irrational. But many people in God's Word had every reason, humanly speaking, to be afraid of their circumstances. They had seen their friends tortured and their family members killed for their faith. They had to face their fears head-on, like many of you.

How did so many of the people of the Bible demonstrate such courage in the face of legitimate danger? What was so special about people like Moses, Jeremiah, Isaiah, Stephen, and Paul? What was their secret?

Here's the key: They had seen God's hand at work. They knew, compared to God and his power, all other enemies were ninety-pound weaklings.

For example, the prophet Elijah faced two ruthless foes in King Ahab and his queen Jezebel who were worthy of the prophet's fear. The preacher R. G. Lee, in his famous sermon "Payday Someday" referred to King Ahab as the "vile toad who squatted on the throne of Israel."

1 Kings 21:25 reads, "There was never a man like Ahab, who sold himself to do evil in the eyes of the LORD, urged on by Jezebel his wife." The queen's depravity was so great that her name has become synonymous with evil.

These two monarchs of Israel once had a man named Naboth killed just because he refused to sell them a vineyard—a plot of land that had been in Naboth's family evidently for generations. The king and queen considered a vineyard more valuable than a man's life! The prophet Elijah could have justified fear and remained silent. He knew that when Jezebel vowed to kill him (which she did), she meant every word.

God informed Elijah what the king and queen had done to Naboth. For Elijah to remain silent would have meant disobedience to God. Elijah courageously confronted King Ahab with his sin and pronounced God's judgment on the king of Israel.

Surprisingly, Ahab temporarily repented of his sin and humbled himself before God. But eventually Ahab and Jezebel both died violent deaths. Elijah, who was faithful to God's calling, was taken up into heaven in a whirlwind by God (see 2 Kings 2:11).

Another Elijah-like prophet lived in the first century. His name was John the Baptist (see Matt. 17:11–13). Like Elijah, John showed more allegiance to the will of God than fear of an evil ruler.

John the Baptist confronted Herod Antipas with his lifestyle of immorality. Herod had committed adultery by taking Herodias, the wife of his brother Philip, as his own. When John confronted the sin of Herod and Herodias, the woman became indignant. She determined to kill John the Baptist.

On Herod's birthday, Herodias instructed her daughter to perform an exotic dance for the ruler. Herod was pleased with the exhibition and promised to give Herodias' daughter anything she wished.

Matthew tells of the request in his Gospel: "Prompted by her mother, she said, 'Give me here on a platter the head of John the Baptist'" (Matt. 14:8). The young woman relayed her mother's request to Herod, and John the Baptist was killed.

Simon Peter's boldness was evident to critics of the gospel. When he overcame his fear of the religious leaders, the change in his life was obvious. Luke wrote, "When [the members of the Jewish council, the Sanhedrin] saw the *courage* of Peter and John and realized that they were unschooled, ordinary men, they were astonished and they took note that these men had been with Jesus" (Acts 4:13, emphasis mine).

Why the drastic difference in courage after the resurrection? Peter trusted more in God who could raise the body from the dead than in human beings who could not keep Jesus in the sealed tomb. Listen to the explanation from Peter himself: "Judge for yourselves whether it is right in God's sight to obey you rather than God. For we cannot help speaking about what we have seen and heard" (Acts 4:19–20). I'd say that about sums it up.

As a matter of fact, look at the disciples' response to pressure and persecution. One might expect the persecuted Christians to pray for protection, or at the very least deliverance. But that's not what these courageous men prayed for. They prayed, "Now, Lord, consider the threats and enable your servants to speak your word with *great boldness*," (Acts 4:29, emphasis mine).

You've got to be kidding me. Boldness? They prayed for more boldness. Why? Their boldness got them into trouble with the officials to begin with. The answer can be seen by noticing how they first addressed God: "Sovereign Lord," they called out (see Acts 4:24).

The disciples knew God was sovereign. Nothing caught him by surprise. In fact, the Romans and religious leaders themselves had played right into the hands of the Almighty. He had used them to bring glory to himself.

How many times have you prayed for God to take pressure away from you or to deliver you from trouble instead of praying for more boldness? Jesus did not come to get us out of trouble. He came to get into trouble with us.

Look at the results of Peter's and John's boldness. God answered their prayer. "After they prayed, the place where they were meeting was shaken. And they were all filled with the Holy Spirit and spoke the word of God boldly" (Acts 4:31).

Before we conclude this portion of our study, I want to ask some questions. Why was Elijah spared and John the Baptist killed? What made the crowd listen to Peter, but turn on Stephen? Why was Paul beaten on some occasions, but released on others? I don't know.

But I do know this: When people choose to seek the approval of God instead of the applause of people, God is glorified, whether the individual lives or dies. The one common thread running through each of these events is that when people overcame their fear of man and courageously stood for God, the Lord was glorified.

What challenge are you facing? What or who is putting pressure on you. Are you facing trouble because you are seeking God's will instead of trying to please people?

If you are facing pressure, what have you prayed for? Deliverance? Safety? Protection? Or courage?

Please allow me to encourage you to practice boldness—not arrogance that comes from personal pride, but heavenly boldness based on the sovereignty of God. He never sleeps or slumbers. He never rests. He never takes a vacation. His eye is on the sparrow, and I know He watches me.

A Godly Legacy for Your Children

Please allow me to say just a word of encouragement to you parents and caregivers of the next generation. May those who follow us in this world find us faithful. Let's communicate to them the importance of overcoming the fear of man and seeking God's approval only.

I wish I could say I've always demonstrated the courage of Christ to my children. I have not. But there have been a few occasions when their mother and I, only by God's grace, have made good decisions and seen positive results.

One summer, Page and I had to make a decision we would rather not have been forced to make. Our summers are spent like many of yours: at the Little League baseball field. With three boys playing ball in three different age groups, it seems like we're at the ball field almost every night of the week.

Due to a baseball game being rained out, our nine-year-old son was supposed to play a makeup game on a Wednesday night during church time. Page and I talked about how we would handle the conflict. It was just for one game. What would it hurt to miss church for one night?

Our family had already made a commitment to worship and to support the ministries of our church on Wednesday nights. What would skipping church to play ball communicate to a nine-year-old about our priorities? What would happen the next time there was a conflict and a decision to be made? So we missed the game.

We knew that some people would think we were being fanatics, or at least a little extreme (some of you might be thinking that yourselves). We tried to explain our decision to the coaches and to others who asked. Some understood and some didn't. That's OK. We had a real peace about our decision.

Truthfully, I don't think it bothered Caleb nearly as much as it did Page and me. But within days, we were affirmed that we had done the right thing.

Just a few days after missing the make-up game, Caleb was running at the ball field and fell on a plastic pipe with jagged edges that was sticking out of the ground. The pipe chewed into the little fellow's leg.

He messed his knee up pretty badly, so I carried him to my truck and rushed him to the MEA clinic in Clinton. While we were in the waiting area, Caleb was on his back on the X-ray table, afraid of the dreaded stitches he knew he was about to receive.

Then my brave son looked up at me through tears and gritted teeth and said, "Dad, we need to pray. Could we have a prayer?" So we did. Immediately, the atmosphere in that room changed. Caleb's spirit was calmed some, and so was mine.

And I'll never forget that time I spent with my son. But you know what? I doubt that he would have responded to that crisis in the way he did if we spent our Sundays and Wednesdays at the baseball or soccer field.

But, parents, you don't make the decision to put a priority on spiritual things on the spur of the moment. You do it from the very beginning when you give the child to the Lord. Then the question is not "What am I going to do?" but "How am I going to be obedient?"

To be honest with you, in some ways the decision to go to church rather than play ball wasn't all that tough. A much more difficult challenge came not long after the incident with Caleb's knee. The next challenge was a lot tougher for me personally, but even more important than the baseball incident in terms of our sons seeing how Page and I would respond.

In order for you to understand our dilemma, I need to emphasize that I am a huge University of Kentucky Wildcats basketball fan. I was reared in the Bluegrass State, and if you were to cut me I would bleed blue. People in Kentucky stick basketball goals on just about anything that doesn't move.

My wife and I were blessed to have some dear friends, Frank and Margarite Singleton, give us tournament tickets and hotel reservations to go to Atlanta for the Southeastern Conference basketball tournament. We were to leave after I finished teaching my last Thursday class and to return after the final game on Sunday afternoon.

The church where we worship and serve was holding a revival the week of the tournament. The revival was going to end on Wednesday night. The tournament didn't start until Thursday afternoon. No problem—we thought.

God poured out his Spirit on the church that week. People were sitting on the floor in the aisles during the services. Relationships were mended. God's people were broken before him. Many were saved. Others recommitted themselves to walk with Christ in every area of life. At least one person I'm aware of committed her life to the mission field.

As God began to work during that week, Page and I knew deep down the revival was going to be extended. You can't put a timetable on the Holy Spirit. Sure enough, the announcement was made: "The revival will be extended through Thursday night."

On the one hand, we thought, "This is wonderful!" On the other we thought, "This is terrible!" What about our plans? What about the hotel room I had already booked? What about the tournament? I'm ashamed now we even had to think about it.

I could hear myself in my imagination saying to the children, "Our relationship with the Lord comes before anything else. He's done so much for us. He's worthy of so much more than we could ever offer him. It's only a ball game." But this was more than a ball game. This was the SEC tournament! This was a preview to March Madness!

The truth is, to hold our children to a standard we were unwilling to live by would have been the epitome of hypocrisy. So, when Thursday night came, we went and worshipped as a family, and God was faithful, as he always is. I'm glad we didn't miss the blessing that night of seeing him once again bless his people. I'll never be the same after that week.

Oh, and the tournament? Well, after the last amen of the worship service on Thursday, Page and I drove all night to Atlanta and were able to get a few hours of sleep before the next round of games began on Friday.

We had a great time—much better than if we had left before the revival was over. And then to top it all off, Kentucky won the tournament the way the Lord intended all along!

I don't expect our children to fully understand the decisions we are making now. But I know one day as they are facing tough decisions on their own, it will be important for them to be able to look back and remember their godly heritage.

Will they make their own mistakes and make poor decisions? Sure—plenty of them. Just like I have. But I hope the general direction of their life is good. We have such a short time. Those little ones, God's arrows, will not be in your quiver long (see Psalm 127).

An Eternal Home in Heaven

"Whoever acknowledges me before men, I will also acknowledge him before my Father in heaven" (Matt. 10:32).

I've saved the greatest reward of all until last. The promise from God of an eternal home with him in heaven is the greatest reward of all for those who live to please our heavenly Father.

Do you ever wonder what goes on in heaven? Ever wonder what Jesus is doing right now? At least some of the time he's preparing a place for you and me to join him one day.

Before Jesus went back to heaven to be with his Father, he tried to ease the troubled hearts of his disciples. Fred Craddock says the disciples were staring at Jesus as children look up at parents who are going out for the evening: asking questions like, "Where are you going?" "When will you be back?" "Why can't we come, too?

So Jesus answered them and said, "Let not your heart be troubled; believe in God, believe also in Me. In My Father's house are many dwelling places; if it were not so, I would have told you; for I go to prepare a place for you. And if I go and prepare a place for you, I will come again, and receive you to Myself; that where I am, there you may be also" (John 14:1–3, KJV).

Recently my family and I attended a college football game with Jerry and Carol Hazelwood. The Hazelwoods' son, Brian, had been the hero of the game the week before. Brian kicked a last-second field goal to win the game. Knowing the hero made going to the game a special treat for my oldest two sons.

Brian's little brother, Brett, was playing high school football at the time. Brett was being recruited by his big brother's team, the Mississippi State University Bulldogs. During half-time, Brett took my sons, his two little "recruits," all of eleven and nine years of age, to the field house. They met team officials and had refreshments. You would have thought my two boys had just been inducted into the Hall of Fame.

After the game, the actual high school recruits, who were given name tags at half-time, were allowed to go onto the field to meet the players. Brett tried to take my boys onto the field with him. But they were so small they were left behind in the rush to the field. Then they were forced to talk their way through a guard at the gate. They must not have looked like hot prospects to the guard. He denied their request to go onto the field.

The rejection deflated the spirits of the little fellows. Their heads dropped toward the ground. Their shoulders drooped. Then, Kyle, the older of the two boys, noticed that the people going onto the field were wearing name tags just like theirs. He realized, "Hey, we're wearing tickets to get in!"

In a moment of youthful courage, Kyle, normally the spokesman for his younger siblings, turned and approached the security officer one more time. Confidently, yet respectfully, Kyle pointed to his name tag and said, "Sir, do we have to be wearing one of *these* to get in?" "Oh, you have name tags," the man replied, impressed. "Come right in."

The lesson I want you to see is this: My sons didn't do anything to earn entrance onto that football field. They were allowed to come in solely on the achievements of another— namely Brett Hazelwood. Because they were with him, their names were written where it counted.

And the best part was, they had a relationship with the hero. They were allowed to celebrate the victory because of the achievements of another. So are we.

You and I didn't do a single thing to inherit the kingdom of heaven. Jesus did it all. He is the hero of salvation. And what matters most is not that our names are written in earthly record books, but that they are recorded in God's record book in heaven.

The ancient emperor Nero was known for his huge spectacles in the Roman Coliseum. Legend has it that one of the most thrilling moments among those activities occurred when the Roman wrestlers marched out.

The wrestlers represented the cream of the crop among the Roman forces. They were the strongest, the quickest, the most agile, the best of the best. When they entered the arena, they marched shoulder to shoulder as one man. The ground shook as they thundered into the coliseum in front of thousands of cheering spectators.

As these warriors advanced, they testified to their allegiance to Nero in unison: "We are wrestlers for you, O Emperor. We will win for you the victory and from you the victor's crown." And the colossal structure shook as these athletes shouted out the anthem.

During the war with Gaul, Nero received news that many of his polished troops, some of whom were these same Atlas-like wrestlers, had professed faith in Jesus and become Christians. Nero had made his hatred of Christians and their movement obvious to all of Rome. In response to the report of many allegedly following Christ, Nero passed an edict: anyone calling themselves Christian would be executed.

The report of the edict eventually reached a centurion named Vespazien. He gathered the troops under his command and read them the decree. To these burly warriors, the best Rome had to offer, Vespazien added, "Now all who after hearing this will still cling to the faith of Christians, step forward."

Vespazien's heart sank at their response. Just as they had marched into the coliseum together, with one stride, together as one man, without hesitation forty of the wrestlers stepped forward.

The centurion tried to reason with them. He pleaded, "I don't want to execute you. You should not die. You are the best. You are the strongest. You are the noblest." Vespazien tried to give them every chance to change their minds—to renounce their faith in Christ. He said, "I'll give you until sundown to change your minds."

The day passed, and the command was repeated by the centurion. But the forty soldiers stood faithfully. They refused to renounce their faith in Christ. With a broken heart, Vespazien gave the official order: "You must be executed."

After issuing the order to execute the Christians, legend has it that Vespazien added, "But I will not have your fellow soldiers spill or shed your blood." So, in the dead of winter, he stripped them of their clothing and marched all forty men onto an inland frozen lake near the place they had set up camp.

Just as they had marched onto the arena floor of the coliseum, now these same courageous warriors for Christ fell in stride. They marched naked onto the ice to die of exposure to the bitter elements.

As they marched again as one man onto the ice, they began to chant in unison: "We are wrestlers for you, O Christ. For you we will win the victory, and from you the victor's crown."

The chant went on and on throughout the frozen night: "Forty wrestlers for you, O Christ. For you we will win the victory, and from you the victor's crown." At moments during the night, the chant grew faint, but on it went.

Then, just before daybreak, the light from the campfire exposed a shivering silhouette making its way toward the shore from the ice. One lone, overexposed soldier had given up. This one soldier was willing to renounce his faith in Christ for the warmth of the Roman Empire.

About the time Vespazien saw the man approaching, he again heard the chant. Their voices had grown dim in the waning hours of the morning. But now the volume picked up once again as the men said, "Thirty-nine wrestlers for you, O Christ. For you we will win the victory, and from you the victor's crown."

What happened next is the most fantastic part of the story. No one is certain what happened to the centurion at that point, but something took place inside this man's heart. All night long he had witnessed the courage and faith of these brave soldiers of Jesus.

Vespazien tore off his own clothes, threw them aside, and sprinted onto the ice, shouting as he ran, "Forty wrestlers for you, O Christ. For you we will win the victory, and from you the victor's crown." The officer traded in his Roman citizenship, considered precious to most people, for citizenship in heaven.

The converted soldier, Vespazien, was echoing the words of the apostle Paul, "Now there is in store for me the crown of righteousness, which the Lord, the righteous Judge, will award to me on that day—and not only to me, but also to all who have longed for his appearing" (2 Tim. 4:8).

This world is not our permanent home. We are just passing through. Isn't that wonderful news? The apostle Paul wrote, "But our citizenship is in heaven. And we eagerly await a Savior from there, the Lord Jesus Christ" (Phil. 3:20).

Why do you think during those moments of deep suffering that you long for something else? God placed that longing inside of us to keep us from putting our permanent anchor down here on the earth.

Peter wrote, "For you know that it was not with perishable things such as silver or gold [see Acts 3:6] that you were redeemed from the empty way of life handed down to you from your forefathers, but with the precious blood of Christ, a lamb without blemish or defect" (1 Pet. 1:18–19).

The promises made by this world will never supply the deepest longings of the human heart. God made us for a higher purpose. He made us to glorify him.

Dennis Rodman recently was asked a probing question during an ESPN interview, "Dennis, you seem to have it all. NBA championship rings, wealth, fame. What more could you possibly want?"

After a brief pause, in a rare moment of transparency, Rodman answered, "Contentment."

No matter how much we accumulate here on this earth, one day it will all be gone. Friends and family members move away or die. Money can be stolen or lose its value. Possessions can rust, wear out, and break. Rich food eventually spoils. Fancy clothes are eaten by moths, if they don't go out of style first.

A wise person makes investments in heaven, where they are more secure than on earth. "In his great mercy he has given us new birth into a living hope through the resurrection of Jesus Christ from the dead, and into an inheritance that can *never perish, spoil or fade—kept in heaven for you,*" (1 Pet. 1:3b–4, emphasis mine).

But in order for you and me to inherit that heavenly home, we must care more about what God thinks of us than what people think. We must confess him as Lord and Savior, even if some people scoff at our confession.

Some will call you a fanatic for thinking about heavenly things. But remember, it is God's approval we long for. And he wants our allegiance. He does not want to share your devotion with anyone. He loves you that much.

This principle of our citizenship being in heaven has huge implications for our lives right now. When we become Christians, we aren't to quit our jobs (unless the job does not honor the Lord), sell everything we have, go sit in the street, and wait for Christ to return.

God still has work for us to do. He has left us on this planet for a reason. He's not finished with us yet. As long as you live, he will have a purpose for you. But primarily that purpose is to bring glory to Him.

In his book, *The Purpose Driven Church*, Rick Warren made an interesting point. He wondered why God left us here on earth. With all the pain and suffering and sorrow in the world, why not just take us right to heaven? He continued telling how we can worship, pray, sing, and hear God's Word in heaven. So why does God leave us here?

I love Warren's answer. He concluded there were two things we can do on earth that we cannot do in heaven. One is sin, and the other is tell lost people about Jesus. Now, which of these two actions do you think God left us here to do?[6]

While we are on the earth, our purpose is to glorify our heavenly Father. But our *ultimate* dwelling place will be with him in heaven. The knowledge and hope of that eternal home motivates us to seek his approval over the favor of any human being.

"Since you call on a Father who judges each man's work impartially, live your lives *as strangers here* in reverent fear" (1 Pet. 1:17, emphasis mine).

Prayer

Holy Father, you give the best gifts. I desire more than any human being can give. I desire your blessing. If you choose to reward my faithfulness with blessings on earth, thank you. If you choose instead to wait until eternity, I praise you all the more.

In many ways I long to be in your presence forever. But I realize you have a purpose for me. I know I will be a citizen of this world only for a short while. While I am here, I pledge my allegiance to you.

Thank you for my dual citizenship. My real home, my permanent home, is in heaven with you. I can't wait to see the place you are preparing for me. Until I move in, please give me the grace I need here on earth to be faithful to your calling. In the name of your Son, Amen.

Chapter 7
A Life That Glorifies the Father

*They came to him and said, "Teacher, we know you
are a man of integrity. Your aren't swayed by men,
because you pay no attention to who they are; but you
teach the way of God in accordance with the truth."*
(Mark 12:14)

*"I do not accept praise from men, but I know you. I
know that you do not have the love of God in your
hearts. I have come in my Father's name, and you do
not accept me; but if someone else comes in his own
name, you will accept him. How can you believe if you
accept praise from one another, yet make no effort to
obtain the praise that comes from the only God?"*
(John 5:41–44)

Jesus Changed the World Forever

The life of Jesus of Nazareth changed the world more than
any event in human history. No event, person, or thing has had
the same impact as the life of Jesus on this earth. He always did
the absolute will of his heavenly Father.

If Jesus' primary goal had been to please people instead of the
Father, he would have been just another good teacher. But Jesus
was unique. As is cited in Mark 12:14, even Jesus' critics recognized he was not intimidated by others.

A few years ago I heard about a publisher who gathered a panel of twenty-eight famous educators and historians and gave them an unusual assignment. They were to list what they believed to be the one hundred most significant events in history.

The event getting the most first-place votes was the discovery of America. Second was the invention of movable type by Gutenberg. Eleven events tied for third place, and four tied for fourth: the invention of the airplane, the innovations of ether and X-ray, and the life of Jesus of Nazareth. Jesus tied for fourth.

With all due respect to the distinguished panel of experts, I stick with my original statement: no event, person, or thing has had the same impact as the life of Jesus on this earth. "[Jesus] is before all things, and in him all things hold together. . . . so that in everything he might have the supremacy" (Col. 1:17–18b).

The impact Jesus has had on our world is nothing short of miraculous, especially considering the age in which he lived. No telephones, no fax machines, no Internet, no satellite communication systems. No frequent flyer mileage for Jesus. He walked everywhere he went. I love the way one author depicted the accomplishments of Jesus given the circumstances in which he lived:

One Solitary Life

He was born in an obscure village, the child of a peasant woman. He grew up in another village, where he worked in a carpenter shop until he was thirty. Then for three years He was an itinerant preacher. He never wrote a book. He never held an office. He never had a family or owned a home. He didn't go to college. He never visited a big city. He never traveled two hundred miles from the place he was born. He did none of the things that usually accompany greatness. He had no credentials but himself.

He was only thirty-three when the tide of public opinion turned against him. His friends ran away. One of them denied him. He was turned over to his enemies and went through the mockery of a trial. He was nailed to a cross between two thieves. While he as dying, his executioners gambled for his garments, the only property he had on earth. When he was dead, he was laid in a borrowed grave through the pity of a friend. Nineteen centuries have come and gone, and today he is the central figure of the human race.

All the armies that have ever marched, all the navies that have ever sailed, all the parliaments that ever sat, all the kings that ever reigned, put together, have not affected the life of man on this earth as much as that one solitary life.[1]

Please forgive me for repeating myself, but I can't say it enough: Jesus turned our world upside down. Of all the characteristics of Jesus recorded in the Gospels, one trait consistently leaps from the pages: Jesus chose obedience to the Father over the approval of human beings—always. So Jesus' life and ministry provides several lessons that will help us overcome our need for the approval of people.

The first way Jesus of Nazareth can help you and me overcome our fear of man is by setting us free with his gift of salvation. We've discussed in a previous chapter how a person is saved by God's grace through his Son. But if you still have not taken this first step by confessing your sins to God and believing in Jesus for forgiveness, you need to stop and do it right now.

Please go back to that section, sincerely pray the prayer at the end of the chapter, and ask Christ to set you free. If you don't take this first step, nothing else matters.

God is not impressed with "good" deeds, but he is pleased with a humble heart. "This is the one I esteem: he who is humble and contrite in spirit, and trembles at my word" (Isa. 66:2b).

In David's confession, the king wrote, "For Thou dost not delight in sacrifice, otherwise I would give it; Thou art not pleased with burnt offering. The sacrifices of God are a broken spirit; A broken and a contrite heart, O God, Thou wilt not despise" (Ps. 51:16–17, NASB).

If you desire a transformation that will enable you to live to please God rather than people, you must give your life completely to the Lord. No outside motivation can create the transformation we need. The permanent change we need must be an inside job. This transformation takes place as God's Holy Spirit takes up residence inside of you.

God can certainly pick you and me up when we fall and when we fail. But his desire is that we not fall in the first place. Jude referred to God as the one "who is able to *keep you* from falling" (Jude 24, emphasis mine).

When you give your life completely to God, he strengthens you "with power through his Spirit in your inner being, so that Christ may dwell in your hearts through faith" (Eph. 3:16–17a). In a moment, we'll discuss the importance of following the example of Jesus, but before he becomes our example, he must become our enabler. Apart from him, we can do nothing (see John 15:5).

After the Holy Spirit transforms your life, he enables you to live a life that glorifies our heavenly Father. He transforms our thinking by giving us the mind of Christ. When your mind is transformed, "then you will be able to test and approve what God's will is—his good, *pleasing,* and perfect will" (Rom 12:2, emphasis mine). In other words, in order to live a life that hears the applause of the Father, you must first be given the mind of his Son.

Then, after we have been transformed, you and I can follow Jesus' flawless example. What did Jesus do? What attitudes did he possess that helped him always hear the sound of God's applause? To keep his priorities straight? How did he do it?

Let's discover together the keys to Jesus' success in glorifying the Father. If we consistently demonstrate these same actions and attitudes, we will be on our way to being liberated from the fear of man. We will be closer to receiving an ovation from heaven.

Constant Contact with the Father

No matter where Jesus was, no matter what he was doing, no matter what difficulties he faced, he was aware of God's constant literal presence—always. For Jesus, God was not the personification of goodness, like Uncle Sam is the personification of democracy. The constant companionship of God was not just a lofty ideal to Jesus, his perfect Son. The presence of the Almighty was not the wishful thinking of a Jewish carpenter. Jesus *knew* he was never out of the Father's presence.

Have you ever heard someone pray for God's presence? As far as I know, Jesus never prayed for the Father to be "with him." So why do we? Our motives may be sincere, but if God's Holy Spirit dwells inside us, there is no need to ask for God to provide his presence. He *is* with us.

When we ask God for his presence, I know what we usually mean. We usually mean, "Lord, please manifest yourself so I can be reminded you are with me," or "Father, please empower us with your grace, to be up to this challenge," but we pray these words: "Lord, be with us." Could it be that we pray for God to "be with us" because we don't have a constant awareness of his presence the way Jesus did?

John's Gospel includes a discourse Jesus gave to his disciples that demonstrates Jesus' constant awareness of his heavenly Father's presence. After Jesus and his disciples completed their last meal together, they began to walk across the Kidron Valley, making their way to the Garden of Gethsemane, where Jesus was later arrested.

While making the transition from the upper room to the garden, Jesus talked to his disciples and then prayed for them. Compare the confident discourse and prayer of Jesus concerning the presence of God (which Jesus spoke primarily for the benefit of others who were listening), with our weaker prayer for God to be with us. Jesus said, "But a time is coming, and has come, when you will be scattered, each to his own home. You will leave me all alone. *Yet I am not alone, for my Father is with me*" (John 16:32, emphasis mine).

Even though Jesus was facing death and knew his friends would abandon him, he was not afraid that he would be alone.

He assured them he would never be alone, even if they all left him. After Jesus' arrest, the Gospel of Mark adds, "Everyone deserted him and fled" (Mark 14:50). Even so, Jesus still experienced the presence of God.

After Jesus talked with his disciples, he prayed to his Father. He prayed for himself, for his disciples, and for all believers in the future. John wrote, "After Jesus said this, he looked toward heaven and prayed: 'Father, the time has come. Glorify your Son, that your Son may glorify you. For you granted him authority over all people that he might give eternal life to all those you have given him'" (John 17:1–2). How about that? The only reason Jesus wanted to be glorified was so he could glorify God.

Then, after praying for the Father to be glorified, Jesus prayed for his disciples: "I am coming to you now, but I say these things while I am still in the world, so that they may have the full measure of my joy within them. . . . My prayer is not that you take them out of the world but that you protect them from the evil one. . . . As you sent me into the world, I have sent them into the world" (John 17:13, 15, 18). In other words, Jesus wasn't sending them into the world alone. Just as the Father accompanied Jesus, so he would provide companionship to the disciples.

Finally, after Jesus prayed for himself and for his disciples, he prayed for you and me: "My prayer is not for them alone. I pray also for those who will believe in me through their message, that all of them may be one, Father, just as you are in me and I am in you. May they also be *in us* so that the world may believe that you have sent me. I have given them the glory that you gave me . . . Father, I want those you have given me to be with me where I am, and to see my glory, the glory you have given me because you loved me before the creation of the world. . . . I have made you known to them, and will continue to make you known in order that the love you have for me may be in them and that I *myself may be in them*," (John 17:20–22, 24, 26, emphases mine).

Enough said. If you belong to Christ, his Spirit lives within you. We don't have to beg him for his presence. He is always with us.

This awareness of God's presence can give present followers of Christ the same confidence and peace experienced by the Savior. To his discourse recorded in John's Gospel, Jesus added, "I have told you these things, so that in me you may have peace. In this world you will have trouble. But take heart! I have overcome the world" (John 16:33). Later Jesus promised, "And surely I am with you always, to the very end of the age" (Matt. 28:20).

Imagine the courage we would have if we were aware of the presence of God *every* moment of *every* day. One summer afternoon I was with my family at a local swimming pool. At the time, my son Kyle was just a little guy and was trying to shoot a basketball at a goal in the pool.

I watched Kyle for a few minutes from a distance. Then several bigger kids swam up, took the ball from him, and shoved him aside. Immediately, I did what most of you parents would have done. I walked over to where they were and punched the biggest kid right in the nose (*not really*—I just wanted to see if you were paying attention.). Actually, I just sat down on the edge of the pool with my legs dangling in the water and began encouraging Kyle to shoot the ball in the basket.

All of a sudden, Kyle became very bold. He didn't cry. He didn't swim away. He didn't hide. He retrieved the ball and shot it toward the basket. Why was he so bold all of a sudden? I had been watching from a distance all along. But before I intervened and reminded Kyle of my presence, he was timid, perhaps even a little afraid.

When I revealed myself, the fear left. And eventually, so did his adversaries. The psalmist referred to our heavenly Father as "our refuge and strength, an *ever-present help* in time of trouble" (Ps. 46:1, emphasis mine). God's presence enables you and me to demonstrate the same courage that Jesus showed.

The writer of Psalm 46 added, "Therefore we will not fear, though the earth give way and the mountains fall into the heart of the sea . . . The LORD Almighty is *with us*; the God of Jacob is our fortress" (Ps. 46:2, 7; emphasis mine).

For Jesus, this consistent awareness of God's presence resulted in a passion for glorifying God. I suppose someone could say, "Yeah, but Jesus is God's Son. We expect him to always be aware of his Father's presence." If we have the attitude that Jesus possessed an unfair advantage over us by being God's Son, we are mistaken. God's Word says, "For we do not have a high priest who is unable to sympathize with our weaknesses, but we have one who has been tempted in every way, just as we are—yet was without sin" (Heb. 4:15).

In fact, one could argue that Jesus' level of temptation was greater in some ways than ours, and Jesus never gave in. When you and I give in to temptation, the pressure is relieved, at least temporarily. Jesus never gave in. Can you imagine the intensity of his temptation in the wilderness? He went forty days without eating. After Jesus had fasted and prayed to the Father, Satan approached him and tempted him to turn a stone into bread. But Jesus resisted.

Then came two more temptations from Jesus' adversary. More pressure. But Jesus resisted, and the devil left him. Luke adds, however, that Satan left Jesus only for a season. The NIV says the devil left Jesus "until an opportune time" (Luke 4:13), implying there would be another day for Satan to attack God's son.

Jesus isn't the only person in Scripture to live under the awareness of God's presence. In the fourth chapter of 2 Timothy, Paul wrote, "At my first defense, no one came to my support, but everyone deserted me. . . . But the Lord stood at my side and gave me strength, so that through me the message might be fully proclaimed and all the Gentiles might hear it" (2 Tim. 4:16–17).

During Paul's ministry, many stood at the apostle's side—fellow soldiers, co-laborers, fellow bond servants. But on this one occasion, when he needed an advocate, someone to speak in his defense, they all left him. Some left Paul for good reasons, like Titus perhaps, to go on missionary campaigns. Others left for painful reasons, like Demas, who loved the world more than his mission for Christ (see 2 Tim. 4:10).

Paul was not bitter toward those who left him. He even hoped the Lord would not hold their abandonment of Paul against them (see 2 Tim. 4:16). And Paul's first desire was not for God to save his life. This champion of the gospel simply wanted to be able to glorify the Father by proclaiming the good news. And he knew God would be glorified, because the Lord stood at his side.

Jesus, the apostle Paul, and many others glorified their heavenly Father and heard the sound of God's applause, in part because they practiced the presence of their heavenly Father. And so can you and I.

Living under the Watchcare of the Father

It's easy to see this principle demonstrated in Scripture. But why is it so hard to live daily with the awareness of God's presence? Why do we normally remember God *after* we've blown it or *after* we've been anxious or afraid?

The answer has several facets. I can think of at least three valid reasons why you and I have difficulty living under the constant watchcare of the Father.

The first reason sounds simplistic, and I suppose it is. The reason you and I have to be reminded of God's presence is that your problems and difficult circumstances involve things and people you can see and touch. We can do neither with God—he is invisible. We have to see the Lord through the eyes of faith. But we can do it with his help.

Do you remember what the author of the "faith chapter" (Heb. 11) wrote about the faith of Moses? Hebrews 11:27 says

Moses believed God, persevered, and stood fearlessly against Pharaoh because he saw him who is invisible.

Moses was over eighty years old by the time he led the Hebrew people to the Promised Land. I don't know how good his physical eyesight was, but his spiritual vision was 20/20. Moses knew that without the perpetual presence of God he would fail, and the stakes were too high to take that risk.

Let's listen to a conversation between God and Moses. In this conversation, Moses admitted to God his helplessness without the Lord's presence. The LORD replied, "My Presence will go with you, and I will give you rest."

Then Moses said to him, "If your Presence does not go with us, do not send us up from here. How will anyone know that you are pleased with me and with your people unless you go with us? What else will distinguish me and your people from all the other people on the face of the earth?"

And the LORD said to Moses, "I will do the very thing you have asked, because I am pleased with you and I know you by name" (Exod. 33:14–17).

Moses lived a life that glorified the Father. He longed for the presence of the Lord on a day-to-day basis. So desperate was Moses for the constant presence of God, he told the Lord, "God, if you don't go with me, I'm not going. If you don't provide your presence in my life, I'd just as soon not live. I want you to be pleased with me. Nothing else matters. Please show me your glory."

God honored Moses' plea. Moses took God at his word. Moses wasn't perfect, but he knew when to hush and trust God. God promised Moses his permanent presence, and Moses believed. After God promised Moses he would always be with him, Moses never begged God for his presence again.

During Moses' long journey through the wilderness with the Hebrew people, Moses heard his share of murmuring and complaining from those he led. But he succeeded in his mission, because he had trained his ears to listen for the sound of God's applause. And one way God provided that ovation was by assuring Moses that he would never leave him alone.

Earthly Distractions

The second reason we have difficulty practicing the presence of the Father is that we become distracted by things or people. These diversions might not be bad in themselves, but when we allow them to take up our time and attention to the detriment of our time alone with the Father, we're asking for trouble.

I really struggle with distractions in my life right now. Like many of you, I like having access to the "toys" we have at our fingertips. We say the notebook computers, fax machines, and cell phones make our lives easier, but they don't. In many ways, these items have complicated our lives. The truth is, we just like the stuff. I'm guilty, just like some of you.

So what am I saying? Should we get rid of all these things and let the world pass us by? No. We could get rid of all the gadgets, and we wouldn't necessarily be any more spiritual. Selling your computer won't allow you to be one step closer to heaven. The issue is not our possessions, but our priorities.

We don't have any more demands on our time than Jesus did. People tugged at him from every direction—children, sick people, people searching for answers to the questions of life. But time alone with the Father remained a priority for the Son—especially when he wanted to remind himself what he came to the earth to do and whose applause he was after.

Jesus told a parable that's recorded in Mark 4 about a farmer who sowed some seed. In the parable, the seed fell on various types of soil. Jesus later explained that the ways the various types of soil responded to the seed represented the way some people respond to the Word of God.

One type of person, Jesus explained, is like seed sown among thorns. In the parable, the plants that sprout among the thorns are choked out by the thorns and do not bear any fruit. Jesus explained how some people hear God's Word, but the message gets choked out by *"the worries of this life, the deceitfulness of wealth, and the desires of other things"* (Mark 4:19, emphasis mine).

Jesus didn't just teach this principle of simplicity. He lived it. The Lord didn't concern himself about owning a chariot with "power everything." He walked everywhere he went.

Jesus didn't fret because he didn't have a new outfit for a special occasion. He owned one seamless robe, and the soldiers gambled for it while he was being crucified.

Jesus never was troubled because his neighborhood was going down and he was concerned about a depreciating home. He didn't have a place to lay his own head (see Matt. 8:20).

On at least one occasion, a multitude of people wanted to change Jesus' simple lifestyle. The event is recorded in John 6. John narrated Jesus' miracle of turning five barley loaves and two small fish into a feast for over five thousand hungry listeners. What a miracle! After every person had eaten his or her fill, Jesus' disciples gathered up more food than they had started with.

The people were amazed when they saw the miraculous sign. They were ready to force Jesus to be their king right then and there. Imagine having a king who could wipe out famine in one day. Some make campaign promises they cannot keep, but Jesus could live up to any claims.

Jesus knew in his heart that they intended to force him to be an earthly king, but that was not his mission. His Father had sent him for a greater purpose: not to appease our physical appetite, but to satisfy our spiritual hunger.

Now, please look at how Jesus responded to the crowd. He didn't try to argue with them. He didn't thank them for their flattery and their compliments of his ability. He did what he often did. He shut out the world's applause and listened once more to the voice of the Father.

"Jesus, knowing that they intended to come and make him king by force, withdrew again to a mountain by himself"

(John 6:15). There you go. That's good counsel for you and me as well. When people start telling you how wonderful you are, get alone and listen to the voice of God. And when people ridicule you, or question your leadership, or scoff at a decision you have made, remember why you are here.

Our purpose for being on this earth is the same as Jesus' purpose: to glorify the Father. To hear his applause—not to attract the approval of the crowd.

The Effects of Unconfessed Sin

A third reason we don't always feel the power of God's presence is because sin short-circuits our communication with the Father. Ever since the first man and woman sinned, sin and the guilt associated with it have affected our day-to-day relationship with God.

Peter, in his first letter, wrote, "Husbands, in the same way be considerate as you live with your wives, and treat them with respect as the weaker partner and as heirs with you of the gracious gift of life, *so that nothing will hinder your prayers*" (1 Pet. 3:7, emphasis mine). Did you notice the last part of that verse?

If I am disobedient to God's instruction regarding the respect I show (or don't show) to my wife, my prayer life suffers. That truth sure explains the apparent ineffectiveness of some of my prayers. Just after James encouraged his readers to confess their sins to one another, he wrote, "The prayer of a *righteous* man is powerful and effective" (James 5:16b, emphasis mine).

Even though Jesus reconciled sinful human beings to our loving God, sin still affects our fellowship with God until we deal with it God's way—that is, until we confess the sin before him and change our behavior.

As I was growing up, when I had been disobedient to my dad, the last thing I wanted to do was spend a lot of time with him. First, spending time with him reminded me of my disobedience. The guilt would eat away at my insides. Second, I knew my dad could see right through me. I didn't want to face the consequences of my disobedience.

When a Christian is disobedient to God, he or she will experience guilt. When we feel guilty, we're tempted to withdraw from God or to run away from him. Running away and ignoring our sin aren't options. God loves us too much to let us go.

Running didn't work for Jonah, and it won't work for you and me if we are God's children. Perhaps your relationship with the Father is suffering right now because of unconfessed sin in your life. Why don't you allow God to deal with the issue right now, before you go any further. I promise you, you will be glad you did.

The Price Jesus Paid for Our Forgiveness

I've deliberately saved the following comments for the last part of this section. Jesus never experienced the guilt we go through because of our sin. He was never out of fellowship with his heavenly Father. His prayers were never short-circuited because of disobedience to the will of God.

Jesus was not distracted by the worries of the world or the deceitfulness of wealth. He never gave in to the flattery and accolades of the crowd. He was aware constantly of the presence of God since his vision was not blurred by any of the things that distract us.

But there was one time in the life of Jesus, just for a few moments, where he did express abandonment by his heavenly Father—on the cross. For three hours, from about noon until 3 P.M., the sky was dark. Matthew 27:46 reads, "About the ninth hour Jesus cried out in a loud voice, . . . 'My God, my God, why have you forsaken me?'"

When we come to the cross, we are on holy ground. I'm certain I will never understand all the implications of Christ's suffering and death. I don't know to what degree Jesus felt grief and abandonment during that moment when he expressed being forsaken by his Father.

Isaiah wrote, "But he was pierced for our transgressions, he was crushed for our iniquities; the punishment that brought us peace was upon him, and by his wounds we are healed" (Isa. 53:5). And to conclude the chapter, the prophet added, "For he bore the sin of many, and made intercession for the transgressors" (Isa. 53:12b).

I have no clue what it must have been like for the perfect Savior of the world to take on the filth of my sin. But one thing I do know—up to that point Jesus had always expressed certainty that he and the Father were one.

The only time in his life where Jesus ever expressed being abandoned by his heavenly Father was when he deliberately made it possible for you and me to experience the permanent presence of God's Holy Spirit in our lives. God answered Jesus' prayer, "I have brought you glory on earth by completing the work you gave me to do. And now, Father, glorify me in your presence with the glory I had with you before the world began" (John 17:4-5).

God gave back to his Son what his Son gave up to come to the earth. But before Jesus was glorified by God, he felt abandonment as a result of the weight of our sins. I'm glad he paid the price.

Because Jesus took our sins on his shoulders, we can experience the constant presence and power of God right now. He always has his eyes on you. "For the eyes of the LORD range throughout the earth to strengthen those whose hearts are fully committed to him" (2 Chron. 16:9a).

One of my favorite choruses captures the joy we can experience when we enjoy the presence of the Lord with other believers:

In the midst of his children,
The Lord said he would be.
It doesn't take very many,
It can be just two or three
And I feel that same sweet Spirit

That I've felt 'oft times before.
Surely I can say that I've been with the Lord.
Surely the presence of the Lord is in this place.
I can feel his mighty power and his grace.
I can hear the brush of angel's wings.
I see glory on each face.
Surely the presence of the Lord is in this place

One rainy day, my wife and my little girl, Gené, went to see a friend of ours named Gina. They arrived at Gina's house just as the rain stopped and the sun came out. God painted a beautiful rainbow across the sky. My daughter's eyes were filled with wonder.

Several days later, Page and Gené went back to Gina's. Page had forgotten completely about the rainbow, but Gené remembered. Gené asked, "Where we goin', Mommy?"

"We're going to Miss Gina's house," Page answered.

Then Gené asked, "Is she going to have another rainbow for us?"

Page smiled. Gené was naive enough to think there should be a rainbow just for her when she visited her friend. God has not promised us he will always provide a rainbow. But he has promised us he will always provide his presence.

God opened the eyes of Elisha's servant, and the servant saw the hills full of God's horses and chariots of fire sent to protect God's people. I want to encourage you with the same words Elisha spoke to his servant: "Don't be afraid. Those who are with us are more than those who are with them" (2 Kings 6:16). You and I have the promise of God's presence. He is all we need.

A Healthy Fear of the Almighty

Some fear is good. Hebrews 5:7 reads, "During the days of Jesus' life on the earth, he offered up prayers and petitions with loud cries and tears to the one who could save him from death, and he was heard because of his reverent submission." The King James Version translates that phrase *reverent submission* as "fear."

Part of living a life that pleases the Father is having a healthy fear, awe, and reverence for him. We *can* fear God and love him at the same time, because he is good, just, faithful, and trustworthy.

This healthy fear of God should lead us to have thankful hearts that he loves us and wants our total allegiance. "Therefore, since we are receiving a kingdom that cannot be shaken, let us be thankful, and so worship God acceptably with reverence and awe, for our 'God is a consuming fire'" (Heb. 12:28–29).

In *The Lion, the Witch, and the Wardrobe*, one of the books in C. S. Lewis's series, The Chronicles of Narnia, one of the characters asks about the Lion, a character who represents Christ, "Is the Lion safe?"

And the answer given is, "No, the Lion is not safe, but he is good." By the same token, God is not safe, but he is good.

It's possible for fear to save us from harm or even death. A loving parent is able to show a child compassion and authority at the same time. For example, when I tell my tiny daughter to stay out of the road, I'm not trying to be mean. I'm trying to help her reach her next birthday in one piece. She may want to chase a ball or a puppy that's gone into the road. Her pursuit might get the ball back. But it wouldn't be safe.

When faced with the above situation, my daughter has to make a decision: *Should I do what is fun, or should I obey my daddy and stay out of the road?* Choosing disobedience may result in discipline. Discipline will result in some form of pain or conflict. In my daughter's moment of decision, possibly a split second, I hope she will choose obedience, for the good of our relationship, and for her own well-being. But if she chooses to be disobedient, I must lovingly discipline her.

I would not be a loving Father if I allowed my child to engage in dangerous activity without addressing the activity. When her life is at stake, a healthy fear of her father could save her. So it is with a healthy fear of God. The psalm of David reads, "As a father has compassion on his children, so the LORD has compassion on those who fear him. . . . From everlasting to everlasting the LORD's love is with those who fear him" (Ps. 103:13, 17a).

Some of you might be thinking, *"Now, wait a second, Hughes. I thought God was a loving God, full of mercy and grace. Doesn't the Bible say that perfect love drives out fear?"*

Yes, God is full of compassion and mercy. He has blessed us with his grace and forgiveness. But when we have a real sense of God's awesome nature and power, a legitimate response is to have a sense of fear. Jesus said, "Do not be afraid of those who kill the body but cannot kill the soul. Rather, be afraid of the One who can destroy both soul and body in hell" (Matt. 10:28).

That's where grace comes in and takes away our fears. God is always faithful and consistent. He is not untrustworthy, unpredictable, or capricious. When you and I are faithful, we have no reason to fear. "In this way, love is made complete among us so that we will have confidence on the day of judgment, because in this world we are like him. There is no fear in love. But perfect love drives out fear" (1 John 4:17–18a).

John Newton's life was changed dramatically because of his fear of God. Newton was born into a Christian home, but his parents died when he was six years old. He eventually ran away from the relatives who had taken him in. They mocked his faith. After becoming an apprentice seaman in the British Navy, he ran away from home, by his own admission, "to sin his fill."

Newton fled to Africa where he was taken in by a Portuguese slave trader who also mistreated the young sailor. The trader's wife made Newton eat off of the dirty floor like a dog.

He left the trader's home and was picked up by a slave ship sailing toward England. Because of his navigational skills, he was made the ship's mate. During the voyage, he broke into the supply of rum and became drunk with the other crew members.

In a drunken stupor, Newton fell overboard. One of the officers managed to save Newton's life by spearing him with a harpoon. For the rest of his life, Newton was reminded of that occasion by a fist-sized scar in his thigh.

Finally, toward the end of the voyage, the ship and crew encountered gale force winds. The ship began to sink and Newton was sent below with the slaves to man the pumps.

Newton worked the pump for days, certain they were doomed to die in the tempest. But while in the hold of that ship, he began to remember the Bible verses he had learned as a child. The grace and love of God swept over him, and he was saved in the belly of that ship.

Newton later became a famous preacher in England. He eventually tried to describe in his own words how God had changed his life. His words put to music have become the most loved hymn of all time. Please allow me to share the words to the second verse of *Amazing Grace* with you. They describe how God's grace led to both fear and forgiveness for this lost soul.

> *'Twas grace that taught my heart to fear,*
> *And grace my fears relieved;*
> *How precious did that grace appear*
> *The hour I first believed!*

In other words, God's grace stirred a holy fear in Newton's heart. Then, God's grace took away the fear. What a relief! What a testimony! What a Savior!

Careful Attention to God's Reputation

There is another reason Jesus was able to live a life that glorified his Father. He was more concerned about God's reputation than his own.

God's *character* has never changed. He's always been the same. But in the first century, some people had dragged God's reputation through the mud. Some taught that God loved only a particular group of people. Others believed God's grace could be earned by following the traditions of their ancestors.

Jesus came with a different message. His message was that no one could afford the price of God's grace, but God would give his grace freely to all who humble themselves before him and believe in his Son.

One of my college professors, Dr. Ray Frank Robbins, used to say, "When Jesus glorified the Father, he raised God's reputation up to be equal to his character." In fact, the word used for "glory" in the New Testament, *doxa*, literally means "opinion." Regarding Jesus' giving glory to the Father, the term means that we have the *right* opinion of God's nature. Jesus said, "If you want to see what God is like, look at me." Jesus paid the ultimate price to make certain our opinion of God's character was accurate.

While Jesus remained in heaven with his Father, the Son's reputation was untarnished. The angels knew who God's favorite was. In heaven, Jesus never heard insults about being a drunk or a "friend of sinners" (see Matt. 11:19). While at home with his Father, Jesus didn't have to hear his critics make snide allegations, questioning his parents' marital status when he was conceived (see John 8:41). While in heaven, Jesus was never accused of being possessed by demons (see John 8:48). But while on earth, Jesus' critics accused him of all of the above and more.

In heaven, Jesus enjoyed an immaculate reputation, just like his Father. On earth, however, the story was different. But that was OK with Jesus—as long as the Father was glorified. As long as the reputation of God was consistent with his character.

The apostle Paul wrote, "[He] made himself of no reputation" (Phil. 2:7, KJV). Literally, that verse says that Jesus emptied himself. Jesus was equal with God, but he put his own reputation aside, so you and I would know how much God loves us and wants to spend eternity with us.

Think about the long journey of Jesus from heaven to earth. He started out equal with God and humbled himself to put on human clothing. That should be enough, shouldn't it? No.

He became not only a human being, but a Jew—one of a despised race of people. If he had been born into a Roman family, at least he couldn't have been crucified—Roman citizens were exempt from the shame of a cross. Jesus didn't have that luxury.

And Jesus wasn't born to an upper-class Jewish family in a beautiful home. No, he was born into a blue-collar home. Instead of a bed with nice clean sheets, a feeding trough filled with hay was his first bed. Nothing flashy about Mary and Joseph. But they were people of faith.

Jesus even gave up the simple lifestyle of Galilee when he grew up. He left home to begin an itinerant ministry of teaching and healing the hurts of people. He didn't have a place of his own where he could put up his feet at night. *Jesus made himself of no reputation.*

Then, when Jesus had finished the work the Father had assigned for him, he gave up his life voluntarily. Jesus died in the prime of life. But not just any death. Crucifixion was the lowest form of death and humiliation one could experience. Crosses were reserved for the most hardened, incorrigible criminals.

In some ways, it would have been surprising if God had *not* chosen the lowest means of death for the one who emptied himself in every way possible. Jesus was even placed in a borrowed tomb.

When Jesus died, Satan must have thought, *There, that should be the end of this "King of Glory" (Ps. 24:7).* But that wasn't the end. It was only the beginning. Jesus was humbled, but look how God exalted him.

God gave back to Jesus the glory, the reputation, that Jesus had given up. "Therefore God exalted him to the highest place and gave him the name that is above every name, that at the name of Jesus every knee should bow, in heaven and on earth and under the earth, and every tongue confess that Jesus Christ is Lord, to the glory of God the Father" (Phil. 2:9–11).

Our purpose for being placed on this earth is not to build our own reputation, or to make a lot of money, or to impress people with our accomplishments. Our one purpose for living is to glorify God with our lives—to raise his reputation to be consistent with his character.

The other day I was watching an episode of *The Andy Griffith Show*. In this episode, two story lines were being developed at the same time.

In one of the plots, Andy tried to deal with the pride of a woman named Anna Belle Silbey. Anna Belle was left by her husband Tom, but she was too proud to admit she had been abandoned. So she told the townspeople Tom had died. She even staged a funeral to make his demise look authentic.

Then one day, Tom showed up in town. Andy told Tom and Anna Belle they should admit to everyone the mistakes they made and get on with their lives. But their pride made their confession difficult.

At the same time Andy was trying to work through the Silbey's dilemma, he was dealing with some confusing behavior by his son, Opie. The resolution of this problem is the second story line of the episode.

The town officials of Mayberry were taking up a collection for the Underprivileged Children's Fund. Andy tried to encourage Opie to give something, but Opie refused. He told his Pa that he was saving his money to buy a birthday present for his girlfriend, Charlotte.

Finally, Opie gave in and gave a few cents to the children's fund. The sheriff wasn't satisfied by his son's token gift. Andy scolded his son for his selfishness. Then he told Opie something like this: "Well now, ain't this a fine how-do-you-do? How do you think it must look to the citizens of Mayberry for the sheriff's son to be giving a few pennies to the children's fund? Some big spender you are." (The audience can tell Opie is hurt because his father is disappointed in his decision.)

By this time in the story, Aunt Bea had heard enough. She confronted Andy about his immature and hypocritical behavior. She told Andy he wasn't concerned about the underprivileged children as much as his reputation.

Andy had ridiculed Anna Belle Silbey because of her pride. But he was blind to his haughty attitude. After he apologized to Opie for being so harsh, Andy asked his son, "Just what is so important for Charlotte to have that you would refuse to give to the children's fund? What are you going to give her for her birthday?"

To which Opie replied, "I'm going to give her a coat, Pa. Hers is all worn out."

During supper that evening, Andy turned down Aunt Bea's fried chicken. He told Aunt Bea he was eating crow instead.

That episode hit home for me because I could hear myself saying some of the same words as Sheriff Taylor. When I was a pastor, I can remember saying (either to myself or my wife and children), "Here I am the pastor of the church; everybody knows who I am, and my child does so and so, or says this or that? What are people going to think? What about my reputation?" Yeah, what about it?

My reputation is not important. God's is.

John the Baptist had the same attitude as Jesus concerning his reputation. John valued Jesus' reputation more than his own. At the same time John the Baptist's influence was diminishing, Jesus' ministry was expanding. In fact, some who once had followed John began to follow Jesus. John wasn't concerned about his reputation. He said, "The reason I came baptizing with water was that he might be revealed to Israel. . . . He must become greater; I must become less" (John 1:31b; 3:30).

When we care more about God's reputation than our own, he will applaud us. He is ready to glorify you, the same way he exalted his Son. Jesus said, "For whoever exalts himself will be humbled, and whoever humbles himself will be exalted" (Matt. 23:12).

Confidence in the Future

The LORD is for me; I will not fear;

What can man do to me?

The LORD is for me among those who help me;

Therefore I shall look with satisfaction on those who hate me.

It is better to take refuge in the LORD

Than to trust in man. (Ps. 118:6–8, NASB)

Jesus also heard the sound of God's applause as a result of his absolute confidence in who determined his future. Jesus understood his future was in the hands of his heavenly Father. Jesus knew no one could take his life from him. God would determine when the time had come for his death. Jesus would not go to the cross one second before the appointed time.

On several occasions, Jesus' adversaries wanted to take his life, but they were unsuccessful. A mob tried to lynch the Lord, but he slipped through the crowd unnoticed. His adversaries tried to stone him but failed.

Even when Jesus' future looked hopeless, humanly speaking, he trusted the Father for the outcome. After Jesus had been arrested, he stood before Pilate. The responsibility to sentence Jesus fell in the lap of the cowardly governor of Judea.

During part of Pilate's interrogation of Christ, Jesus gave Pilate no answer. Pilate blasted back, "Do you refuse to speak to me? Don't you realize I have power either to free you or to crucify you?"

Jesus' answer to the governor was brief and to the point: "You would have no power over me if it were not given to you from above" (see John 19:11a). Jesus answered to a higher authority than an earthly governor.

Consider what Jesus said about the Father and the Son being one. Since God is the ultimate authority over everything and everyone and since Jesus was God in the flesh, wouldn't that mean Jesus had given the authority to Pilate in the first place?

The Lord told his disciples, "All authority in heaven and on earth has been given to me" (Matt. 28:18). In Romans 13:1, Paul wrote, "There is no authority except that which God has established."

Does this mean God causes people like Adolph Hitler to rise to power and terrorize the world? No. It means, no matter how evil or powerful people are, human beings cannot usurp the authority of God and prohibit his ultimate will from being done.

Jesus was confident about the future, even when the future looked dark. This confidence that his future was in the hands of the Father enabled Jesus to be courageous in the presence of his accusers. And the Father was pleased.

Our future is not determined by what happens in Washington, D.C. What lies ahead for you is not determined by your boss or the board or the city council. No human being holds your future in his or her hands. God does. "The LORD foils the plans of the nations; he thwarts the purposes of the peoples. But the plans of the LORD stand firm forever, the purposes of his heart through all generations" (Ps. 33:10-11).

How foolish we must appear to God when we try to please others instead of him, because we believe those people somehow can help or hurt our future. In this regard we can learn a valuable lesson from Job's experience.

I hope you never suffer the way Job did. He lost his family, his house, even his health. But he never lost his faith. Even his wife told Job to curse God and die, but he refused. His friends mocked him and shook their heads at his pitiful condition.

Job's "friends" accused him of sinning against God. "That's why God is judging you. You've made him angry," they charged. "Admit your guilt. Maybe he will have mercy on you, Job." Job wasn't perfect, but there was no besetting sin in his life to deserve all the pain he was going through. No, something else was going on, but Job wasn't certain what it was.

Finally, Job began to break down. He never cursed God, but he threw a pretty big "pity party" (I don't know about you, but

I would have been ready to give up long before Job did). Let's listen in when Job longed for the days before catastrophe struck his life: "How I long for the months gone by, for the days when God watched over me, when his lamp shone upon me head and by his light I walked through the darkness!" (Job 29:2). God hadn't gone anywhere, but at the time, he seemed a long way from Job.

Then as Job's discourse continued, Job's thoughts turned to his own reputation. His suffering affected others' opinions of him. "When I went to the gate of the city and took my seat in the public square, the young men saw me and stepped aside and the old men rose to their feet; . . . Whoever heard me spoke well of me, and those who saw me commended me" (Job 29:7–8, 11). Can you blame Job for being discouraged? He had once been a respected man of influence in his community. Now he was a laughingstock.

God allowed Job to pine away. He allowed Job, Job's friends, and his wife to have their say. Then the Lord had had enough. After the Father listened to his servant's grieving, the Lord spoke. God said, "Are you finished, Job?" (that's a genuine Hughes paraphrase). "If you are finished, I have something I would like to say. I'll speak and you *will* listen." By the way, God always has the last say. And when God spoke, Job listened.

The Father asked, "Who is this that darkens my counsel with words without knowledge? . . . Where were you when I laid the earth's foundation? Tell me, if you understand. Who marked off its dimensions? Surely you know! Who stretched a measuring line across it?" (Job 38:2, 4–5).

> Have you ever given orders to the morning, or shown the dawn its place? . . . Have you journeyed to the springs of the sea or walked in the recesses of the deep? . . . Surely you know, for you were already born! You have lived so many years! (Job 38:12, 16, 21).

Job was a smart man. He got the picture. God had a plan and a purpose for Job's life. Job's perspective was limited. Job realized God was more interested in his character than in his comfort level. So even though Job's circumstances were terrible, his attitude changed. He understood God's plan was perfect.

Job answered the LORD, "I am unworthy—how can I reply to you? I put my hand over my mouth. I spoke once, but I have no answer—twice, but I will say no more." . . .

> "I know that you can do all things; no plan of yours can be thwarted. . . . Surely I spoke of things I did not understand, things too wonderful for me to know" (Job 40:3–5; 42:2, 3b).

God accepted Job's apology and exalted Job. He restored his reputation before Job's peers, and he made Job prosper twice as much as before. The conclusion of the story reads, "The LORD blessed the latter part of Job's life more than the first. . . . And so he died, old and full of years" (Job 42:12a, 17).

Maybe you can identify with Job. Maybe you can't. What matters is that you are aware God has a plan for your life and no human being can thwart those plans without God's permission.

Jesus' faith in the Father's plan enabled him to focus on eternal matters, not on temporal things. Jesus knew nothing or no one could harm him without the Father's permission. Some people call this confidence in God's ultimate plan a "but if not" kind of faith.

The phrase "but if not" comes from the story of the three Hebrew young men who would not bow down to the ninety-foot golden idol of Nebuchadnezzar, the king of Babylon. King Neb thought he controlled the destiny of the brave young men. They knew better. They knew their future rested in the hands of God.

The three young men were named Shadrach, Meshach, and Abednego. They told the king, "If we are thrown into the blazing furnace, the God we serve is able to save us from it, and he will rescue us from your hand, O king. But even if he does not, we want you to know, O king, that we will not serve your gods or worship the image of gold you have set up" (Dan. 3:17–18).

That's a "but if not" kind of faith. The real measure of faith is not whether we believe when God gets us out of the fire. Genuine faith is being in the fire and believing just the same.

An anonymous Christian gave this testimony:

> God is able to deliver from my
> weariness and pain
> And he will deliver swiftly if it
> be for lasting gain,
> But if not, my heart shall sing
> Trusting wholly in my King.
> God is able to supply me with abundance
> from his store,
> And he will supply my table with his blessings
> more and more;
> But if not, my heart shall rest
> In the thought that he knows best.
> God is able to defend me from my foes
> who throng around
> And he will defend me surely when their rage
> and hate abound.
> But if not, I'll bless his name
> And confess him just the same.
> God is able to deliver me from all
> my fears within
> And he will both save and keep me in his fold
> safe gathered in;
> But if not, he'll hold my hand,
> Teaching me to understand.

Esther said, "If I perish, I perish" (Esth. 4:16). The apostle Paul wrote, "For to me, to live is Christ and to die is gain" (Phil. 1:21). Jesus, Esther, Paul, and the three Hebrew young men were saying virtually the same thing: "I trust God for my future."

Jesus focused on eternal matters, not temporal things. "He who loves his life loses it, and he who hates his life in this world shall keep it to life eternal" (John 12:25, NASB). He knew how the story would end.

"God is faithful, who will not allow you to be tempted beyond what you are able, but with the temptation will provide the way of escape also, that you may be able to endure it" (1 Cor. 10:13, NASB).

What fire are you facing right now? Pressure to conform at work? Pressure to compromise at school? Are you on a team with people who ridicule you for your convictions? Your success or failure does not depend on the words or actions of others.

If you are being mocked, ridiculed, or shown disrespect because of your desire to please your heavenly Father, I have good news: God will exalt you in his time. He may not respond when you want him to, but he is never late. Sometimes you might think that Satan is winning in your world. Jesus won our victory on the cross. No matter how much the Adversary kicks and screams, he is already defeated.

Leonard Sweet recently visited the campus of Mississippi College and told in chapel about taking a trip to an Amazon River village. A tribal elder in the village told a story to the group almost every night. Usually the story involved snakes. Evidently, there is an abundance of giant anacondas in these little villages scattered along the Amazon. Some of these snakes measure twenty-five feet in length and can swallow a cow whole.

In this particular village a giant anaconda had slithered in and attacked a mother and her small child. By the way, these snakes are not poisonous, so they must constrict their prey until the victim suffocates. The snake literally squeezes the life out of the victim. Then the serpent swallows its meal whole.

As the elder told the story, he mentioned a Quaker missionary who was ministering to the village people at the time of the attack. The missionary ran frantically to his hut and rummaged through his belongings until he found what he had gone after—a pistol.

As the missionary ran back to where the serpent was crushing its victims, he couldn't remember whether he had loaded the gun. He checked the contents of the pistol to discover he had only one bullet in the weapon and did not have enough time to return to his hut for more. He would have to make the one bullet count.

He inched as close as he could to the writhing snake, without putting his life in danger along with the others. In a scene which must have looked like Barney Fife pointing his revolver at a bandit, with trembling hands, the normally nonviolent man tried to steady the pistol right between the snake's eyes. Then he pulled the trigger. Bull's-eye! The bullet found its mark right between the eyes.

But that wasn't the end of the story. It was only the beginning. As Sweet put it, "That's when all hell broke loose." The fatal blow had been dealt, but the fight wasn't over. See, when the missionary shot that giant anaconda, the snake began a seven-hour wreaking of havoc on the tiny village. Before morning it had devastated most of the village. Finally the snake died.

Dear reader, on the cross of Calvary, Satan had the Son of God in his coils, but Jesus was not a helpless victim. In the resurrection, the Son of God dealt a death blow to that ancient serpent. From the cross, Jesus announced the victory: "It is finished!"

Still, the prince of darkness is not going down without a fight. And there are going to be many casualties who will line his path of destruction. Don't be one of them. You don't have to be his victim.

The Book of Revelation tells us the end of the story. God is victorious. Join him by receiving his grace, love, and forgiveness, and escape the coils of the serpent. "So the LORD God said to the serpent, . . . I will put enmity between you and the woman, and between your offspring and hers; he will crush your head, and you will strike his heel" (Gen. 3:14a, 15).

Don't listen to the jeers of people. Listen to the cheers from heaven. Continue to honor the Lord with your words and deeds, and you will hear the sound of God's applause.

"In him we were also chosen, having been predestined according to the plan of him who works out everything in conformity with the purpose of his will, in order that we, who were the first to hope in Christ, might be for the praise of his glory" (Eph. 1:11–12).

Remembrance of a Divine Calling

When Jesus suffered for doing God's will because others didn't approve of what he was doing, he remembered what he was called to do. He remembered how the Old Testament prophets had suffered before him. He knew how the ancient prophets described the suffering of God's servant, the Messiah.

Jesus was not surprised when he suffered for fulfilling his divine mission. He knew his journey back to the glory of heaven went through the cross. When the cross was near, Jesus faced the decision to please God or human beings. In those critical days, Jesus remembered his divine calling—his reason for coming to the earth.

Jesus replied, "The hour has come for the Son of Man to be glorified. I tell you the truth, unless a kernel of wheat falls to the ground and dies, it remains only a single seed. But if it dies, it produces many seeds. The man who loves his life will lose it, while the man who hates his life in this world will keep it for eternal life" (John 12:23–25).

Jesus wasn't aloof or unaware of the severity of his circumstances. He was honest with his disciples about his emotions. But God's call on his life was clear. Disobedience was not an option. Jesus added, "Now my heart is troubled, and what shall I say? 'Father, save me from this hour'? No, it was for this very reason I came to this hour" (John 12:27).

Once again, Jesus' primary goal was to glorify his heavenly Father, not save his own life. He prayed, "'Father, glorify your name!' Then a voice came from heaven, "I have glorified it, and will glorify it again'" (John 12:28).

Now, what about you and me? Well, in order to seek the applause of God and not the approval of people, we must have a clear sense of our calling as children and servants of God.

In the discourse mentioned above, Jesus told his disciples to expect similar treatment from the world. But if they would remain faithful, God would glorify himself in them like he glorified himself in the Son. "Whoever serves me must follow me; and where I am, my servant also will be. My Father will honor the one who serves me" (John 12:26).

Jesus said those who accept the call to be his disciples would suffer persecution in the same way the ancient prophets of God suffered. Many of these prophets, inspired by God's Holy Spirit, foretold how the Messiah would suffer:

> Here is my servant, whom I uphold, (my chosen one in whom I delight; I will put my Spirit on him and he will bring justice to the nations. (Isa. 42:1)

> I offered my back to those who beat me, my cheeks to those who pulled out my beard; I did not hide my face from mocking and spitting. (Isa. 50:6)

Jesus knew only he, as the Father's Messiah, could fulfill the task God gave him. He didn't need people to affirm his work because he had a divine commission. He had the testimony of his Father. Jesus said, "There is another who testifies in my favor, and I know that his testimony about me is valid" (John 5:32).

Like the Lord himself, Jesus' followers dealt with some of their difficulty with people by remembering the predictions Jesus made about how others would respond to them. He said, "If the world hates you, keep in mind that it hated me first" (John 15:18) and "In this world you will have trouble. But take heart! I have overcome the world" (John 16:33b).

Paul's suffering was no surprise to the great missionary and church planter. The Lord predicted the apostle would suffer for the name of Christ. In a vision, the Lord appeared to Ananias and told him how Paul would suffer as a part of his calling. Jesus said, "This man is my chosen instrument to carry my name before the Gentiles and their kings and before the people of Israel. I will show him how much he must suffer for my name" (Acts 9:15–16).

Paul lived a life that glorified his heavenly Father. His call from God meant more to him than human approval. He wrote, "Am I now trying to win the approval of men, or of God? Or am I trying to please men? If I were still trying to please men, I would not be a servant of Christ" (Gal. 1:10).

Paul's commission came from God, not people. And God's purpose was fulfilled in him because God called him. "And we know that in all things God works for the good of those who love him, who have been *called* according to his purpose" (Rom. 8:28).

So, when you are tempted to yield to pressure from people, remember you have been called by God for a higher purpose: to glorify Him. When others try to intimidate you, remember suffering is part of your calling as a follower of Christ.

Previously in our study, we saw how Jesus began the Sermon on the Mount. He instructed his audience on the qualities that bring God's blessing and approval. Jesus ended the Beatitudes with instructions on how to respond to persecution and suffering for doing good. Jesus seemed to be saying, "Now if you demonstrate these qualities of which God approves, get ready. You will be persecuted, but rejoice when that happens. You're in good company. They persecuted the prophets in the same way. They will treat me in the same manner, and if you serve me, they will treat you with contempt, too. But remember, no servant is greater than his master."

Whatever you face, whatever you endure, whatever it takes to answer the call of Christ on your life—please do it. You won't be sorry. You'll be so glad you answered the call of Christ.

From where I stand I may not
see the Master's hand,
yet, day by day his love unveils his master plan.
So I am sure he leads the way, and I will go,
I will obey.
The call of Christ is my one desire,
though sacrifice he may require.
When I am weak he will suffice, in all I seek,
the call of Christ.
No greater goal, no higher prize than
I could hold
is worth the treasure found in giving
him control.
No earthly gain can match the prize,
my only aim the call of Christ.
The call of Christ is my one desire,
though sacrifice he may require.
When I am weak he will suffice,
in all I seek the call of Christ.
The call of Christ is my one desire,
though sacrifice he may require.
When I am weak he will suffice, in all I seek, in
all I claim, my only aim, the call of Christ.[2]

If you and I have been called to be followers of Christ, God will give us the grace to live a life worthy of our calling. God knows what he's doing. Your calling to be his disciple was no mistake. He will enable you to seek his pleasure more than the applause of human beings. "Therefore, my brothers, be all the more eager to make your *calling* and election sure. For if you do these things, you will never fall, and you will receive a rich welcome into the eternal kingdom of our Lord and Savior Jesus Christ" (2 Pet. 1:10–11, emphasis mine).

Polycarp, the second century bishop of Smyrna, was brought before the Roman proconsul and given a choice: renounce his faith in Christ and live, or be faithful to his heavenly calling and be burned at the stake. Polycarp replied, "Eighty and six years have I served him, and he has done me no wrong. How then can I blaspheme my King and my Savior?"

In order to save himself from excruciating pain and death, all he had to do was say Caesar was Lord. But instead of ignoring his call to be a disciple, Polycarp bravely replied, "What are you waiting for? Bring on what you will." And they did.

A Holy Anointing from the Father to Do His Will

In the Old Testament, the kings of Israel were anointed with olive oil mixed with spices, from a special vessel that was kept in the temple. During the first part of the coronation ceremony in the temple, the oil was poured over the king's head, and the people chanted, "Long live the king."

The anointing of the king carried with it authority and special blessing from God for his chosen instrument, the king. People believed the anointed one had direct contact with God.[3]

The high priest was anointed in ancient Israel before entering the Holy of Holies. This was a way for the priest to enter the holy sanctuary purified and undefiled before the Lord. God's anointed ones were set apart by God for a particular purpose: to glorify the Father.

God anointed his One and Only Son as his representative to do his will. Jesus announced the Father's anointing on his life in the synagogue in his hometown of Nazareth. While some people were afraid to follow him for fear they would be excommunicated from the synagogue, Jesus embraced the opportunity to glorify his Father.

While in his hometown synagogue, Jesus was handed the scroll of Isaiah the prophet, and he read, "The Spirit of the Lord is on me, because he has anointed me to preach good news to the poor. He has sent me to proclaim freedom for the prisoners and recovery of sight for the blind, to release the oppressed, to proclaim the year of the Lord's favor" (Luke 4:18–19).

After reading the scroll, Jesus rolled it up, gave it back to the synagogue attendant, and sat down. Every eye in the place was fixed on Jesus in anticipation of what he would say next. Then he broke the silence by announcing, "Today this scripture is fulfilled in your hearing" (Luke 4:21b). Jesus finished his remarks with a rebuke of his listeners for their lack of faith.

Jesus' audience became furious. They drove him out of town and tried to force him off a cliff. But he was able to slip through the crowd unnoticed, and he went on his way (see Luke 4:28–30).

What a contrast there was between Jesus' courage regarding the synagogue and the cowardice of others. This is just one more example of how Jesus regarded the seal of God's approval more desirable than the approval of human institutions.

As he read from the scroll of Isaiah, Jesus said, "This is referring to me. I am God's anointed." Even the term *Christ* means "anointed one." With regard to Jesus, God's anointing involved a granting of God's Holy Spirit on his Son. This anointing gave the Son a supernatural power and commission to do the will of the Father.

In Acts 4, after Peter and John were released from prison for preaching about Jesus, they prayed for more boldness to spread the good news. In their prayer, they quoted the words of David in Psalm 2: "Why do the nations rage and the peoples plot in vain? The kings of the earth take their stand and the rulers gather together against the Lord and against his Anointed One" (Acts 4:25–26).

If you and I are going to live lives that glorify the Father and hear his applause, we must live with the boldness that is ours by being his anointed people. When you and I take on the name of Christ and become *Christ*ians, we identify with Jesus and his anointing as well. John wrote, "But you have an anointing from the Holy One, and all of you know the truth. . . . As for you, the anointing you received from him remains in you, and you do not need anyone to teach you. But as his anointing teaches you about all things and as that anointing is real, not counterfeit— just as it has taught you, remain in him" (1 John 2:20, 27).

Have you received the anointing of God's Holy Spirit? God's anointing isn't something extra that comes in addition to salvation. When God saves a person by his grace, the person is anointed with God's Holy Spirit right then.

Have you *remained in him*? Even though you and I receive God's anointing as those set apart to glorify him, there is a sense that we need periodic fresh encounters and touches from him to give us a fresh sense of his anointing.

When was the last time you thanked God for his anointing on your life? Can you remember the last opportunity you took to be broken before the Lord and ask him for a fresh encounter with his Holy Spirit? A renewed sense of his anointing?

At a recent pastor's conference I attended, Jim Cymbala shared from his heart the work God was doing at the Brooklyn Tabernacle, where he and his wife Carol have served for the past twenty-five years. With sincere humility and faith, Jim closed out the final session of the pastor's conference by glorifying God for the changed lives they've witnessed in the "city that never sleeps."

I've been to many conferences like this one. I've heard wonderful preaching and inspirational singing, but there was something special about that night, and I want to tell you about it.

Jim admitted he doesn't have a lot of seminary degrees or academic credentials. He seemed truly surprised that God had used him and the people of the Brooklyn Tabernacle in such a unique way, and even more surprised that he was now telling his story to thousands of pastors and spouses as the final speaker of the conference.

Please allow me to tell you what I sensed during that conference. Academic credentials or not, Cymbala has an anointing on his life and ministry that all the doctorates in the world can't provide. As he led us in worship, he demonstrated an uncommon freedom to follow the leading of the Holy Spirit. We were all blessed.

During most of these conferences, especially as the hour grows late, as was the case that evening, people leave by the scores before the end of the meeting. Even when well-known, gifted speakers and worship leaders are on the program, people file out of the convention hall.

But they didn't budge the evening Cymbala spoke. I was sitting in the middle of the hall, but everyone I spoke to after that evening said the same thing: "I didn't see anyone leave while Cymbala was speaking." That's almost a miracle in itself.

We were on the edge of our seats as we watched a video presentation about the changed life of one man who had been touched by God through ministry of the Brooklyn Tabernacle. Through technology we walked the city streets of New York. We visited the place where this former crack cocaine addict had slept in an abandoned car. We walked up to the foundation of the house where he used to buy his drugs. We met his precious wife and children who prayed for hours that God would save their daddy's life and bring him home to them. God heard and answered their prayers.

Then this former inhabitant of the streets, now a citizen of heaven, sang a song entitled "I'm Clean." He was indeed. When Cymbala shared about this man's story and the changed lives of many others, everyone listened intently.

Most of us were asking ourselves the same question that night: *I wonder if God could use me like that? There are so many who need his touch. I wish I had that kind of courage. I'd like to see results like that.*

Well, just remember, those kinds of results don't come without a price. Cymbala, his family, and the people of the Brooklyn

Tabernacle have been through fiery trials as well. Remember, they've been in the trenches for twenty-five years.

The main reason for sharing this event with you is because I wanted to tell you what happened at the end of the worship experience that evening of the conference. Pastor Cymbala shared from his heart the "secret" to what God was doing in their community. It was no real secret. According to Jim, prayer had been the key to witnessing God glorifying himself in fresh, new ways.

He continued by explaining some reasons he believed more churches weren't seeing God's hand at work in similar ways in their communities. There is no way I can recreate for you the atmosphere of that meeting. But if I were to summarize everything he said, I would put it like this: "Quit trying to tell the Holy Spirit what to do, and be obedient to what he is saying to the church and to individual believers. Instead of asking God to bless our agenda, ask for insight about His agenda and then trust him to see it through." In other words, stop trying and start trusting.

When Jim Cymbala began talking about having a hunger for a fresh anointing and a new touch from God, I could sense that those who were there were resonating with each word. Finally, he concluded by giving an odd, but appropriate, invitation.

As his wife, Carol, played the organ in the background, Cymbala invited anyone to publicly come to the front of the auditorium and ask God for a fresh touch and a fresh anointing from him. He wasn't manipulative. Actually, he didn't say a whole lot. He just gave the invitation and stepped back while the Holy Spirit began to work.

Thousands stood and began to flood to the front. Ministers and others from all over the building walked toward the platform, most of them falling to their knees spontaneously when they arrived.

As I made my way to the front, I saw my brother-in-law Chip, who is a young pastor, taking a place among the others to pray.

I thought I would slip in beside Chip and perhaps have a time of prayer with him during this special moment.

But when I arrived at the front of the auditorium and made my way around the first row of chairs, I saw a flash of white go by in front of me. It was Mike Gilchrist (his white mane stood out in the partially dark auditorium), the seasoned evangelist to whom I introduced you in another section of this book. (He was robbed at gunpoint at a post office, remember?)

I stopped long enough to have a brief prayer with Mike, then I slipped in behind Chip. The front of the auditorium was beginning to get crowded by this time, and someone was already beside him. We continued to pray, and Cymbala asked us, if we felt led, to just reach over to someone beside us and say a prayer for them. He encouraged us to pray for a fresh touch from God's Holy Spirit, to pray for insight and direction, and to pray a divine blessing on the other person's ministry.

I looked up to see Chip already praying with a gentleman who was kneeling next to him on that concrete floor. The man was dressed in a suit, but he was on his knees with his face and hands facing the floor, as if he was bowing. I turned around to see a teenage young man kneeling behind me. He was alone, so I placed my hand on his shoulder and prayed for him.

After I said, "Amen," the blond teenager looked up with a half-smile and said, "Thank you." Then I turned around once again toward the front. The time of prayer was coming to an end by this time, but the worship service wasn't over. Jim Cymbala asked all of us in that convention hall to stand and lift our voices in song as we thanked the Lord for all his goodness.

We all stood and began singing "Amazing grace, how sweet the sound, that saved a wretch like me." Everyone joined hands as we sang. I was standing between Chip and the man he had been praying for. As we joined hands and sang, people all over the building spontaneously lifted high their joined hands in thanksgiving to the One who had called them into ministry.

Finally we lowered our hands as Cymbala concluded the service, and I noticed who was standing to my right. The man who had been kneeling beside Chip, the one my brother-in-law prayed for, was Adrian Rogers, pastor of the Bellevue Baptist Church in Memphis, Tennessee. Pastor Rogers is a successful preacher and author and has been for most of my lifetime. The auditorium was dark, and I hadn't paid any attention to who was next to me. Later, Chip told me he hadn't recognized Adrian Rogers until we stood, either. He was just praying for a brother.

Before we left the building, Cymbala encouraged us to find several people and give them a big hug (men with men and women with women) and encourage them in the Lord. So when the lights came up, Pastor Rogers embraced me and said, "God bless you, brother. God bless you and keep you. God bless your ministry."

I have never met Adrian Rogers formally. I don't know anything about him apart from his ministry at Bellevue. But seeing this successful pastor humble himself before the Lord and ask God for a fresh touch from his Holy Spirit was encouraging to this young preacher.

Since that conference, I've thought about the differences and similarities of the people I saw in those few moments in the front of that auditorium:

Mike Gilchrist, full-time evangelist for some forty years, still going strong. Nothing to prove, but still seeking the Lord's face for direction and power.

Adrian Rogers, successful pastor and author. Endeared by man because of a long-time ministry where God has planted him. Still sensing his constant need to humble himself before the one who called him.

Chip Henderson, serving his first church since graduating from the seminary. A gifted preacher with a precious family and a promising future. Acknowledging his need for God's presence and power. How can he not succeed?

The blond-haired teenager whose name I don't even know. Remembering his Creator in the days of his youth. He's facing some difficult days as a teenager in the nineties. Young people have to grow up too quickly in our culture. But he will never have to walk alone.

And then there was me, thirty-eight-year-old preacher and teacher. Just getting started, really. Desperately asking for God's hand to be at work in everything I do. I can identify with Moses, "If your Presence does not go with us, do not send us up from here," (see Exod. 33:15).

Four distinct people with unique gifts but a shared calling to serve where God places us and to do what he wills for us. We are never too young to ask for his anointing and blessing. We never will become so successful or so experienced that we don't need regularly a fresh touch from the Holy Spirit.

On the evening of the pastor's conference, I saw demonstrated a principle I knew was true. But the principle was demonstrated in a new way to me. From a human perspective, some of us in that conference hall were "successful," and some had not "arrived" yet. But we all needed and longed for the same touch of God's hand that night. What's the principle? *The ground is still level at the cross.*

If you belong to Christ, no matter who you are, he has anointed you as his chosen instrument to glorify him. Without him we can do nothing. Without his anointing, we will never live a life that glorifies the Father. But with his anointing, we have supernatural power to say no to pleasing people and yes to pleasing our Father in heaven.

Conclusion

❧❧❧

In the classic movie, *Chariots of Fire*, Eric Liddell had to make a choice between winning the approval of many of his fellow Britons or glorifying God with his athletic gifts. Liddell was a twenty-two-year-old world-class Scottish sprinter who was a favorite to win the Olympic gold medal in his best event, the one-hundred-meter run.

In the movie, Eric's sister, Jenny, pleaded with Eric to follow in their father's footsteps and minister in their mission in China, instead of running for worldly glory. She gently chided him saying, "I'm frightened for you, Eric—frightened for what it might do to you."

Liddell struggled with his decision and then announced his plans to Jenny. He told her he had decided to go to China, but he had some running to do first. He was going to Paris for the 1924 Olympic Games.

As it turned out, the tough decisions were not over for the young Scottish sprinter when he decided to go to Paris. After arriving in Paris, Eric learned that the qualifying heats for the event in which he was the favorite to win were being held on Sunday, the Lord's Day. He refused to run.

Officials and diplomats, from his own coach to the Prince of Wales, tried to convince Liddell to run on Sunday, even though to do so, for Eric, would go against his convictions about participating in athletic events on the Lord's Day. He didn't compromise.

Finally, a team member, who respected Liddell for his convictions and his character, offered Eric the chance to take his place and run in another event. Eric was not the favorite in the four-hundred-meter run, but he could run for God's glory and not compromise his convictions.

Just before the race, an admirer handed him a slip of paper with a note: "In the old book it says, 'He that honors me I will honor.'" In one of the classic scenes in the film, Liddell was in full stride, preparing to stretch toward the finish line when he remembered his conversation with Jenny. His own words rang in his ears, as they still echo in mine. He said, in that charming Scottish brogue, "I believe that God made me for a purpose—for China. But he also made me fast, and when I run I feel his pleasure."

Eric Liddell won the gold medal in Paris that day. But that's nothing compared to the treasure he laid up in heaven. He died in occupied China shortly after World War II, but years earlier he received his "Approved unto God" degree in France.

Liddell's use of his life and stewardship of his athletic ability is a wonderful example of how our purpose is to honor our heavenly Father in whatever we do. Just like God had a plan for Eric Liddell, he created you for a purpose. And he made you fast. When you "run," figuratively speaking, do you feel his pleasure?

When you live day to day, do you feel God's pleasure? As with most analogies, there is one major area where the example of Liddell's race breaks down. For most of us, life is not a sprint; it's a marathon. We're in it for the long haul. All the more reason to run it for the glory of God.

I've heard the tradition of carrying the Olympic torch originated in the ancient Olympic games in Greece. In the ancient games, instead of one torch being carried, every marathon runner carried his own torch. The goal of the athlete was not only to finish the race. The challenge was to cross the finish line still holding the burning torch.

Our goal in life is not to finish first. Our purpose is not to make a big bang and then fizzle out toward the end. Our goal is to glorify our Father in heaven and then to cross his finish line with our torch still burning for Jesus Christ. That takes patience, but marathons aren't won by sprinters.

> Yet those who wait for the LORD
> Will gain new strength;
> They will mount up with wings like eagles,
> They will run and not get tired,
> They will walk and not become weary.
> (Isa. 40:31 NASB)

Prayer

Father, I'm not a flashy sprinter. I want to run for you, but I want to do it over the long haul. I want to begin my pilgrimage with you well, but more importantly, I want to cross the finish line with my torch still burning. As I arise every day, help me to run for you, to feel your pleasure.

And when my attitudes or behavior aren't pleasing to you, please forgive me. Set my feet back on the right course. By your holy presence let me hear your voice saying, "Press on, my child. Stretch toward the finish line. I'm running with you. If you fall, I'll pick you up. If you stray, I'll let you know. Let your torch burn for me and feel my pleasure."

Amen

What Do I Do Now?

All through the writing of this book I've wondered how I would conclude. How in the world do you draw these ideas to a close? Then the other day, Page was singing a song in the car, preparing to sing a concert that evening. She sang a song I hadn't heard in a long time, but the words beautifully tell the same message I've been trying to communicate:

I'd rather have Jesus than men's applause.
I'd rather be faithful to his dear cause.
I'd rather have Jesus than worldwide fame
I'd rather be true to his holy name.
Than to be the king of a vast domain
Or be held in sin's dread sway
I'd rather have Jesus than anything
This world affords today.[4]

I hope that is your testimony. If you would rather have Jesus than money, fame, or the world's applause, you will live a life that glorifies the Father.

Are you ready to begin the journey? I think I can help you get started. You can begin the same way I did—by repenting of living to please people and surrendering to seeking God's applause. Are you ready? Here's a simple prayer that may help:

> Holy Father, please forgive me of seeking the approval of others over your applause. Right now I repent. I pledge to seek your approval. I promise to seek your will for me. Your blessing means more to me than anything this world offers. I know you will not lead me anywhere without providing your presence. If you are with me, who can be against me?

> Thank you for your presence. Thank you for your power. Thank you for your promises. You made me, and you made me fast. When I run, I want to feel your pleasure. In the name of Jesus I pray.

> Amen

Now, listen closely. Do you hear it? I believe I can hear a heavenly ovation.

Notes

❧❧❧

Introduction

1. Bill Bradley, *Time Present, Time Past* (New York: Alfred A. Knopf, 1996), 191–92.

2. J. C. Watts, quote from speech given at the Southern Baptist Convention's Pastor's Conference, Dallas, Tx., 16 June 1997.

3. David Jeremiah, *The Handwriting on the Wall* (Dallas: Word, 1992), 78–79.

Chapter 1

1. William Barclay, *The Gospel of John* (Philadelphia: Westminster Press, 1955), 155.

2. Del Fehsenfeld, *Fear of Man* (Garland, Tx.: Tim Lee Ministries Video Production, 1989).

Chapter 2

1. John Trent and Gary Smalley, *The Gift of the Blessing* (Nashville: Thomas Nelson, 1993), 1–3.

2. Jill Morgan, *A Man of the Word: The Life of G. Campbell Morgan* (New York: Revell, 1951), 59–60.

Chapter 3

1. Lisa Price, "Little League Player Benched for Taking a Stand," CNN Interactive, 10 July 1998.

2. Hannah Whitall Smith, *The Christian's Secret of a Happy Life* (Uhrichsville, Oh.: Barbour and Company, 1985), 38.

3. Author unknown.

4. Author unknown.

5. Jill Lawrence, "A Politically Correct Early Winter," *USA Today*, 23 December 1997.

6. Charles Colson, *Breakpoint*, a part of Prison Fellowship Ministries, 22 April 1998.

Chapter 4

1. John Stott, *Sermon on the Mount (Matthew 5–7): Christian Counter-Culture*, The Bible Speaks Today Series (Downers Grove, Ill.: Intervarsity Press, 1978), 131–32.

Chapter 5

1. D. A. Carson, *The Sermon on the Mount: An Evangelical Exposition of Matthew 5–7* (Grand Rapids: Baker, 1978), 16.

Chapter 6

1. Bob Russell, *Education Is Not Wisdom,* The Living Word Tape Ministry.
2. In Galatians 2:12–13, Paul explained that Peter was afraid of the circumcision group. He referred to the Judaizers, who attempted to add observance of the Law of Moses to the necessity of faith for salvation.
3. "Let the Walls Come Down," Words and music by Jon Mohr. Copyright ©1991. Jonathan Mark Music. All rights controlled by Gaither Copyright Management. Used by permission.
4. "When I Am Afraid." Birdwing Music, Written by Frank Hernandez.
5. Bob Russell, The Living Word Tape Ministry.
6. Rick Warren, *The Purpose Driven Church* (Grand Rapids: Zondervan, 1995), 116.

Chapter 7

1. Officially the author of "One Solitary Life" is unknown, but some have attributed it to Philips Brooks, the writer of "O Little Town of Bethlehem."
2. "The Call of Christ," words by Randy Vader, music by Jay Rouse, Praise Gathering Publications.
3. Colin Brown, ed., *The New International Dictionary of New Testament Theology* (Grand Rapids: Paternoster Press, 1975).
4. Rhea F. Miller and George Beverly Shea.